THE NOTION OF EMPTINESS IN EARLY BUDDHISM

The Notion of Emptiness in Early Buddhism

CHOONG Mun-keat (Wei-keat)

MOTILAL BANARSIDASS PUBLISHERS
PRIVATE LIMITED • DELHI

First Edition: Singapore, 1995
Second Revised Edition: Delhi, 1999

ISBN: 81-208-1649-8

Also available at:

MOTILAL BANARSIDASS

41 U.A. Bungalow Road, Jawahar Nagar, Delhi 110 007
8 Mahalaxmi Chamber, Warden Road, Mumbai 400 026
120 Royapettah High Road, Mylapore, Chennai 600 004
Sanas Plaza, 1302, Baji Rao Road, Pune 411 002
16 St. Mark's Road, Bangalore 560 001
8 Camac Street, Calcutta 700 017
Ashok Rajpath, Patna 800 004
Chowk, Varanasi 221 001

PRINTED IN INDIA
BY JAINENDRA PRAKASH JAIN AT SHRI JAINENDRA PRESS,
A-45 NARAINA, PHASE I, NEW DELHI 110 028
AND PUBLISHED BY NARENDRA PRAKASH JAIN FOR
MOTILAL BANARSIDASS PUBLISHERS PRIVATE LIMITED,
BUNGALOW ROAD, DELHI 110 007

Foreword

When Choong Mun-keat first told me that he was planning a research project on "emptiness" in early Buddhism, I greeted the proposal with enthusiasm. I was happy to act as consultant during the research; and now that his report on that research has taken shape as a book, I welcome this opportunity to comment on the outcome.

Research of the sort presented in this book is all too rare in the field of Buddhist studies. While the notion of emptiness in Mahāyāna Buddhism has been studied in depth by many competent scholars, the antecedents of that notion in the early Buddhist schools have received little attention. Also, there has been a widespread tendency for such studies of early Buddhist teachings to focus exclusively on what is found in the Pāli Nikāyas, the texts of the tradition that calls itself Theravāda. Such a narrow, one-sided approach has been avoided here, as I will now point out.

Dr. Choong has based his research on comparison of the Pāli Nikāyas with the corresponding texts of other early schools, as represented in the extant Chinese Āgamas. Being translations, mainly from Sanskrit, of the now lost texts of the Sarvāstivāda and other long extinct early schools, the Chinese Āgamas provide valuable material for comparative study. Comparison of the Pāli and Chinese versions of any particular sutra can reveal what is common and what is different. This enables the researcher to distinguish, with some confidence, between teachings that date from the period before the corresponding schools diverged and teachings that developed subsequently. If, for example, a sutra from Pāli Buddhism is compared with its Chinese counterpart from the Sarvāstivāda canon, then one is probably justified in claiming that any shared elements of doctrine date from before the split that yielded the Vibhajyavāda and Sarvāstivāda branches within the Sthavira tradition. Since that split is known to have occurred shortly before the Third Council (mid third century B.C.), one can draw soundly based, though still tentative, conclusions about the antiquity of the pieces of doctrine in question.

What this means, in general terms, is that any study of the early phases of Buddhist doctrinal development should be based not only on the Pāli sutras, but also on their Chinese counterparts. This methodological principle, though recognized by a few Buddhist scholars, is only rarely applied in actual research. That it forms the basis for the study reported here therefore enhances considerably the value of this book. The work presented here is more than a study of an important Buddhist doctrine; it is also an exemplification of a research procedure that ought to be much more widely adopted in Buddhist studies.

Scholars will welcome the care and thoroughness with which the research reported here has been carried out, and the light it throws on early doctrinal developments in Buddhism. And devotees will find in the book not only Dharmic sustenance but also an excellent example of how the methods of the scholar can help elucidate, at least at the intellectual level, the meaning of an otherwise difficult aspect of the Buddha's teaching.

Rod Bucknell

Department of Studies in Religion
and Department of Asian Languages and Studies,
The University of Queensland

Preface to the Second Edition

This book presents an investigation into the teaching of *emptiness* according to the Pāli and Chinese versions of the early Buddhist canon. The second edition of this book has been revised and expanded from the first edition of 1995 (on which the author's name was given as SHI Wei-keat). I would like to express my gratitude to Associate Professor Dr. Rod BUCKNELL for his help in the revision process.

The notion of *emptiness* in early Buddhism is mainly concerned with the practical teaching for attaining in this very life *a mind that is liberated* (P. cittaṃ vimuttaṃ, Skt. cittaṃ vimuktam), a mind totally empty of (free from) affliction or distress. This is an essential teaching, relevant to elimination of "self-attachment" and "the two extreme views", a teaching based on the path of *wisdom* (P. paññā, Skt. prajñā) or *right view* (P. sammā diṭṭhi, Skt. samyagdṛṣṭi). In other words, the notion of *emptiness* in early Buddhism is about *wisdom* or *right view*, which leads to the mind becoming totally empty of self-attachment, empty of the two extremes, and thus attaining the highest peaceful state (nirvana), completely empty of affliction or distress. The teachings of the Buddha in both the Pāli and Chinese versions of early Buddhist texts are therefore said to be *connected with emptiness* (P. suññatā-paṭisaṃyuttā, Skt. śūnyatā-pratisaṃyuktā).

Another topic discussed in the early Buddhist texts is the teaching of *faith*, *confidence* (P. saddhā, Skt. śraddhā) or *definite faith* (P. avecca pasāda, Skt. avetya prasāda). For example, *definite faith* is equated with the *faculty of faith* (saddhā-indriya), which is one of the *five faculties* (P. Skt. pañca-indriyāni: *faith*, *effort*, *mindfulness*, *concentration*, and *wisdom*). Faith in early Buddhist texts is not passionate, fanatical, or blind faith, but is closely related to *wisdom*. "Calmed faith" (P. pasāda, Skt. prasāda), cultivated in daily devotion to Buddha-Dharma-Saṅgha, leads to confidence in and practice of the *five moralities* (pañca-sīla), in which the *stream-enterer* (sotāpanna) should abide. The verbal form of pasāda is pasīdati, which means not only "to have faith", but also "to be clear and calm; to become of peaceful heart; to be purified, reconciled or pleased" (PED, p. 447). Faith, in early Buddhism, is essentially governed and stabilised by "individual understanding". For example, SN 48. 52 records the Buddha as saying:

> Bhiksus (monks), as long as the *noble knowledge* (ariyañāṇa) has not uprisen in the noble disciple (ariyasāvaka), then there is no stability (saṇṭhiti), no steadfastness (avaṭṭhiti) of the [other] four *faculties*. But when the noble knowledge has uprisen in the noble disciple, then, bhiksus, there is stability, steadfastness of the other four *faculties*. (SN v, p. 228)

The corresponding Chinese version, SA 654-656, has similar content (T 2, p. 183; CSA ii, p. 299). The *noble knowledge* refers to the *faculty of wisdom* (paññā-indriya). This *wisdom-faculty* in early Buddhism is entirely individual understanding of the Dharma, or the *wisdom* of *right view*. The two versions here record in common that cultivation of the *wisdom-faculty* is regarded as fundamentally important for the development of the *faculties* of *faith*, *effort*, *mindfulness*, and *concentration*. Thus, *faith* in early Buddhism is clearly not a passionate, fanatical, or blind faith. It is based on individual understanding, the *wisdom* of *right view*; and as mentioned above, this *wisdom* of *right view* is connected with the notion of *emptiness*.

Within Buddhist studies it is widely assumed that only the Pāli texts represent "early Buddhism". Naturally, the Pāli texts are important sources for the study of early Buddhism; however, the Pāli canon, as the scripture of the southern

Buddhist tradition (the self-styled "Theravāda", Teaching of the Elders), belonging to the school Tāmraśāṭīya (or Tāmraparṇīya, the Buddhist sect or monks of Tāmraparṇī), represents only one of the various "early Buddhist schools" (so-called "Hīnayāna Buddhism"). If one only considers and emphasises Pāli sources, without comparing them with the Chinese versions, then one is studying Pāli Buddhism, not early Buddhism. For the study of early Buddhism it is essential to pay attention to both the Pāli and the Chinese versions of the early canon. Therefore, in this book, the references to *emptiness* in early Buddhism cover not only the Pāli texts, but also the Chinese versions representing other early Buddhist schools.

It is my hope that this book may, by providing supportive early Buddhist textual information, help readers to attain a good relationship with "emptiness", to possess confidence in daily devotion to Buddha-Dharma-Saṅgha, and to lead a happy and meaningful life, with stability of mind and loving-kindness.

Wei-keat (CHOONG, Mun Keat)
Veluvana
Brisbane, Australia
June, 1998

Acknowledgments to the First Edition

This book was originally submitted as a thesis for the degree of "Master of Arts in Studies in Religion" in the Department of Studies in Religion, University of Queensland, in November 1994. Its publication as a book has been made possible by the support of Ven. Hui-siong (慧雄). Here I would like to express my gratitude for his support of my academic work.

I would also like to acknowledge gratefully the help I have received from Ven. Miao-sheng (妙勝), who presented me with three volumes of the Taisho Tripiṭaka; Ven. Wei-seng (唯成), who presented me with "Agonbu", *Daizōkyō Sakuin* vol. 1 and *Kokuyaku Issaikyō* vols. 1-5; and Ms. AW-YONG Mui-yin (欧阳梅英), who presented me with the English translations of the Pāli Nikāyas. I also wish to express my great appreciation to Ven. Hui-siong, Ven. Fa-zhao (法照), Ven. Miao-sheng, Ven. Wei-seng, Ven. Ri-heng (日恒), Ms. SUN Jin-lian (孫金蓮) and her family, Ms. AW-YONG Mui-yin and her family, and many others, who supported my study.

Finally, I acknowledge the help of my supervisor, Dr. Rod BUCKNELL, who suggested many improvements in style and presentation. However, any mistakes that remain are entirely my own responsibility

煒傑
Wei-keat (CHOONG, Mun Keat)
Veluvana
Brisbane, Australia
June 1995

Abbreviations

AN	Aṅguttara-nikāya
ASA	Additional Translation of Saṃyuktāgama 別譯雜阿含經
BSOAS	Bulletin of the School of Oriental and African Studies, University of London.
CSA	Combined Edition of Sūtra & Śāstra of the Saṃyuktāgama 雜阿含經論會編
DA	Dīrghāgama 長阿含經
DN	Dīgha-nikāya
EA	Ekottarāgama 增一阿含經
MA	Madhyamāgama 中阿含經
MN	Majjhima-nikāya
SA	Saṃyuktāgama 雜阿含經
SN	Saṃyutta-nikāya
Sn.	Sutta-nipāta
P.	Pāli
PED	Pali-English Dictionary (eds. Rhys Davids & Stede)
PTS	The Pali Text Society, London.
Skt.	Sanskrit
T	Taishō Tripiṭaka 大正大藏經 or Taishōshinshū-Daizōkyō 大正新修大藏經

Table of Contents

Introduction

"Emptiness" is a characteristically Buddhist teaching. The present study is concerned with this teaching of emptiness (P.[1] suññatā, Skt. śūnyatā), as presented in the texts of early Buddhism. Its purpose is to clarify and evaluate the hypothesis that the doctrine of emptiness is not just a creation of early Mahāyāna Buddhism, but appears already in early Buddhist sutras, though not yet as a central notion.[2]

1. Aim of the study, subject matter, and argument

The teaching of emptiness is recognized as the central philosophy of early Mahāyāna. However, this teaching exists in both early Buddhism and early Mahāyāna Buddhism, where it is connected with the meaning of conditioned genesis, the middle way, nirvana, and not-self (P. anatta, Skt. anātman). The word "emptiness" in early Buddhist texts is not used as a special term for a central teaching. In contrast, the *Prajñā-pāramitā-sūtras* of early Mahāyāna emphasise emptiness as a central teaching, repeatedly stating that "all dharmas are empty", and using "emptiness" as a synonym for "nirvana".[3] Also Nāgārjuna (founder of the Mādhyamika school) in his *Mūla-madhyamaka-kārikā* (中論) uses emptiness to express the meaning of the middle way of conditioned genesis;[4] for him, emptiness is the same as conditioned genesis.[5]

It seems to me that this early Mahāyāna emphasis on emptiness as meaning nirvana and the middle way of conditioned genesis is quite different from what we find in early Buddhism. Early Buddhism focuses on observing the nature of life as "impermanent" (anicca) and "suffering" (dukkha), in order to realise that all phenomena are "not-self" (anatta), and thus attain nirvana (nibbāna).

The aim of this study, therefore, is to examine two questions: (1) Was the teaching of the Buddha concerned with the notion of emptiness as was the early Mahāyāna? (2) How did early Buddhism express the meaning of conditioned genesis, the middle way, nirvana, not-self, as they relate to the meaning of emptiness? I shall argue that the teaching of emptiness is not a creation of early Mahāyāna, but that it has clear antecedents in early Buddhism. That is, I shall identify the prototype of the notion of emptiness in Buddhism.

2. Sources and Methodology

There has been considerable research on emptiness in early Mahāyāna, but not much on emptiness in early Buddhism. The reasons for this are: First, the early Buddhist texts *often* state that conditioned phenomena are "anicca" (impermanent), "dukkha" (suffering), "anatta" (not-self), and that realisation of this is the fundamental way to the attainment of nirvana, and they use these three terms as keys to express the central teaching of the Buddha; but they do not use "suññatā" (emptiness) or "suñña" (empty) in this way. Second, although the terms "suññatā" and "suñña" do appear in early Buddhist texts, they usually mean simply "voidness" and "void", or sometimes have the same meaning as "not-self"; they do not denote an essential doctrine, as they do in early Mahāyāna.

In a 1982 article titled "原始仏教における空" ["Emptiness in Early Buddhism"][6] FUJITA Kotatsu provides certain information on emptiness, focusing on how the terms "emptiness" and "empty" appear in the early Buddhist texts; but he is not concerned with the meaning of emptiness, or with why it is relevant to the Buddha's teaching as expressed in early Buddhist texts. In his book, 空之探究 [*A Study of Emptiness*],[7] Yin Shun also provides information on emptiness in Āgama (阿含 Ahan) Buddhism, based on early Buddhist texts. FUJITA and Yin Shun are exceptions. Most scholars researching the teachings of early Buddhism, while discussing "impermanence", "suffering", and "not-self" as a set of central ideas, do not discuss "emptiness". According to Hajime NAKAMURA, studies on the philosophy of early Mahāyāna regard the early Buddhist terms "middle way" and "not-self" as equivalent to Nāgārjuna's "emptiness",[8] and see the Buddha's silence on metaphysical problems as a way of emptiness similar to that which Nāgārjuna uses to wipe out all views (Skt. dṛṣṭi).[9] This assumes that the usage of the term "emptiness" in early Mahāyāna does not come from, or represent, the teaching of the Buddha. Because emptiness is not generally considered a teaching of early Buddhism, there are very limited secondary sources on this subject.

Accordingly, in this investigation into the early Buddhist notion of emptiness, almost the only sources used for research and argument are the early Buddhist sutras themselves.

Representing early Buddhist sutras are the five Pāli Nikāyas and the Chinese translations of the four Āgamas (四阿含經). The five Nikāyas, belonging to the tradition Tāmraśāṭīya "Copper-clad" (i.e. Pāli Buddhism),[10] are as follows: (1) Dīgha-nikāya, (2) Majjhima-nikāya, (3) Saṃyutta-nikāya, (4) Aṅguttara-nikāya, and (5) Khuddaka-nikāya. The Khuddaka-nikāya contains fifteen collections, of which the Dhammapada and the Sutta-nipāta are considered the earliest.[11] Corresponding to the first four Nikāyas are the four Āgamas preserved in Chinese translation, mostly from Sanskrit, as follows: (1) Saṃyuktāgama (雜阿含經), which is the counterpart of

Saṃyutta-nikāya, translated by Guṇa-bhadra (求那跋陀羅) in the fifth century A.D. (two of the fifty fascicles have been lost). (2) Madhyamāgama (中阿含經), which corresponds to Majjhima-nikāya, translated by Saṃghadeva (僧伽提婆) in the fourth century. These two Āgamas are recognised as belonging to the Sarvāstivādin school. (3) Dīrghāgama (長阿含經), which is the counterpart of Dīgha-nikāya, translated by Buddhayaśas (佛陀耶舍) and Zhu Fo Nian (竺佛念) in the fifth century. This text belongs to the Dharmaguptaka school. (4) Ekottarāgama (增一阿含經), which corresponds roughly to Aṅguttara-nikāya, translated by Dharmanandi (曇摩難提) and revised by Saṃghadeva (僧伽提婆) in the fourth century. It belongs to the Mahāsaṃghika school, and already contains Mahāyāna ideas. Besides these, there is a Chinese "Additional translation of the Saṃyuktāgama" (別譯雜阿含經), which is an incomplete translation of part of the Saṃyuktāgama. This text may belong to the Kāśyapīya school.[12]

Most of the texts listed above have been translated into modern languages. For the Pāli texts there exist complete English, Japanese, and Chinese translations, whereas the Chinese texts have only Japanese translations (see bibliography). The present study is directly based on the relevant Pāli and Chinese originals.

The basic formation of the Āgamas and Nikāyas dates from the period of the first and second councils (saṃgīti),[13] which took place before the schism of the early Buddhist schools (i.e. between the demise of the Buddha and about 300 B.C.). Of the texts representing early Buddhist teaching, the Saṃyuktāgama/Saṃyutta-nikāya is now considered by Yin Shun and MIZUNO Kōgen to be the foundation of the other Āgamas/Nikāyas.[14] According to Yin Shun, the common ancestor of the Saṃyuktāgama and Saṃyutta-nikāya was compiled at the first council,[15] and represents "Original Buddhism".[16] I accept this view. The Saṃyuktāgama and Saṃyutta-nikāya are therefore the main textual source for the present research.

Yin Shun points out that the material in the Saṃyuktāgama and the Saṃyutta-nikāya can be recognized as belonging to three types (aṅgas): Sūtra (P. Sutta, 修多羅), Geya (P. Geyya, 祇夜), and Vyākaraṇa (P. Veyyākaraṇa, 記說).[17]

(1) Sūtra or Sutta consists of short, simple prose. Monks at the first council collected the Buddha's teachings under four headings according to subject matter: The Five Aggregates (i.e. Khandha-vagga), The Six Sense-spheres (Saḷāyatana-vagga), Causes-and-Conditions (Nidāna-vagga), and Path (Mahā-vagga). Since the texts are grouped according to subject matter, they are called Saṃyukta/Saṃyutta, meaning "connected with". These represent the earliest teaching, but in the extant texts they have already become mixed with other components that came later.

(2) Geya or Geyya was originally a general term for verse. However, it also refers more specifically to the verse component of SA/SN, i.e. 八衆誦 (Bazhong Song "Eight Assemblies Section") in SA and its counterpart Sagātha-vagga in SN, contrasting with the Sūtra of the other four vaggas. The Sutta-nipāta and Dhammapada, also in verse, are classed as Gāthā and Udāna respectively.

(3) Vyākaraṇa or Veyyākaraṇa, which literally means "answer", "explanation" or "exposition", is of two types: Tathāgata Vyākaraṇa and Disciple Vyākaraṇa. These components are mixed with the Sūtra of the four vaggas. Disciple Vyākaraṇa, presented as the words of disciples rather than of the Buddha, puts emphasis on distinguishing the meaning of the Dharma, and also contains exposition of Geya.

Yin Shun maintains that these three types were formed in the above sequence.[18] Material in verse, such as the Sutta-nipāta, Dhammapada, and Sagātha-vagga developed relatively late; the prose Sūtra material is earlier, and can be taken as representing the earliest teaching of Buddhism.[19] However, one has to recognise that the presently existing Chinese Āgamas and Pāli Nikāyas are not the original texts from the time of the first and second councils. Not only were they collected and compiled at different times, early or late; they also belong to several different schools and are already mixed with components from the early Buddhist schools.

Another important resource for this research was Yin Shun's *Combined Edition of Sūtra and Śāstra of the Saṃyuktāgama*. It is a new edition of the Saṃyuktāgama, divided into the three types (Sūtra, Geya, Vyākaraṇa),[20] with corrections, comments, information on Pāli and other Chinese counterparts, and the commentary, Sūtra-mātṛkā, from the Vastu-saṃgrahaṇī of the *Yogācāra-bhūmi-śāstra* (瑜伽師地論).[21]

Pāli and Chinese indexes and concordances were also very useful tools for this study, particularly *Nanden Daizōkyō Sō Sakuin* (General Index to the Pāli Texts),[22] and "Agonbu", vol. 1 of *Daizōkyō Sakuin* (Index to the Chinese Āgamas).[23]

Accordingly, in doing this research, I pay attention to both the Chinese and the Pāli texts, particularly the Chinese Saṃyuktāgama and the Pāli Saṃyutta-nikāya, without giving preference to either tradition. Quoted selections are translated literally from both these texts. Thus, this is entirely a textual study, as regards both sources and methodology.

3. Presentation

In addition to this Introduction and a Conclusion, the study is presented in two large chapters:

One: The Meaning of Emptiness in Early Buddhism, and
Two: The Practice of Emptiness in Early Buddhism.

In chapter one, I examine

(1) emptiness and the place for practising meditation,
(2) the emptiness of 空三昧 kong-sanmei/suññatā-vihāra[24] (meditative state of emptiness) and empty world (suñña-loka),
(3) conditioned genesis, nirvana and emptiness, and
(4) the recognition of emptiness in early Buddhist texts.

I not only examine how the term "emptiness" appears in the texts of early Buddhism but also seek to explain why and to identify the meaning of the term as it is used.

In chapter two, I examine

(1) emptiness and samatha-vipassanā (calm and insight),
(2) emptiness and mind-liberation or mind-concentration (cetovimutti/cetosamādhi),
(3) emptiness and the three concentrations (samādhī), the three kinds of contact (phassa), and
(4) small and great emptiness.

Since early Buddhism is essentially a practical philosophy, I focus here on the relationship between "emptiness" and meditation practice in early Buddhist texts, looking at *how* (description), *why* (explanation), and *what* (classification).

Chapter One: The Meaning of "Emptiness" in Early Buddhism

1.1. *Emptiness and the Place for Practising Meditation*

In early Buddhism the meaning of emptiness centres on practice and experience rather than idealistic and systematic theory. This becomes apparent when one looks at the meaning of "emptiness" as applied to the location or environment where the monk practises meditation. Early Buddhist texts contain a number of statements linking "emptiness" with "the place for practising meditation". For example, at SN 54.1 the Buddha, referring to ānāpānasati "mindfulness by in and out breathing", says:

> Monks, in this connection, a monk, going to the forest (araññāgato) or going to the root of a tree (rukkha-mūlagato) or going to an empty place (suññāgāra-gato), sitting cross-legged, holding the body straight, setting mindfulness in front of him, mindfully breathes out and in.[25]

"The forest" (arañña), "the root of a tree" (rukkhamūla), and "an empty place" (suññāgāra) are frequently mentioned in early Buddhist texts;[26] these were the most common places for monks to practise meditation.

Suññāgāra, "an empty place", is a lonely place, an uninhabited or solitary spot. Similar to this is suññageha, that is an empty dwelling, hut, or house.[27] In SN 7. 18 "empty" (suñña) and "lonely" (vijana) are used to describe a forest (arañña) as an empty place (suññāgāra) for practising meditation.[28] So, whether applied to a forest or to the root of a tree, the terms suññāgāra and suññageha, refer to lonely, secluded places suitable for a monk to stay and practise meditation. Thus, a suññāgāra or suññageha can be an actual physical place.

Other actual solitary places referred to as empty places (suññāgāra) suitable for practising meditation are pabbata (a mountain, hill), kandara (a cave, grotto), giriguhā (a mountain cleft), susāna (a cemetery), vanapattha (forest-space), abbhokāsa (open space), and palāpuñja (straw-pile).[29] Similar examples can be seen in the Chinese versions, such as MA 182.[30]

In early Buddhist texts the word "suñña" (or "suññaka") sometimes has the same meaning as "ritta" (or "rittaka") and "tuccha" (or "tucchaka"),[31] i.e. it has the common meaning of "empty, void, lonely, quiet, secluded", without any special sense.

Generally, however, going to "an empty place" means going to practise meditation. The resulting freedom from outer disturbance leads to freedom from inner disturbance, stillness of the mind. That mental state, just like the empty place, is described as "empty" or "emptiness". For example, the verse in SN 4. 6 says:

> The sage (muni) who resorts to *empty dwellings* (suñña-gehāni) is excellent, *empty of self* (atta-suññato) ... The great sage who goes to an *empty place* (suññāgāra) does not move even a hair of the body.[32]

Its Chinese counterpart, SA 1089, reads as follows:

> Just like an empty dwelling, the mind of the sage is empty (猶如空舍宅，牟尼心虛寂) ... does not move a hair [of the body] ...[33]

Accordingly, there is a natural connection between the "empty place" where the meditator practises and the "emptiness" of the meditative state which he attains there. The word "empty" or "emptiness", applied literally to the "empty place", is also used metaphorically to describe the meditative state experienced in an empty place. That is, an empty place is where the monk lives while practising meditation; his meditative state is experienced in empty places. And the resulting state of meditation is like the empty place in being free of interruption from the outer world and free of inner affliction in the mind. Thus, the state of meditation is also called "suññatā-vihāra" (abode or state of emptiness) etc.[34] "Vihāra", which is a noun and an adjective from "viharati" (to stay, abide), later becomes a common term for an organised Buddhist monastery, but at the time of the Buddha it also means an abode in the forest or a hut, a secluded habitation for a monk.[35] Hence, the state or realm of meditation is called a "vihāra" (abode), and this is its usage in the term "suññatā-vihāra" and others.

In other words, the term "suñña" in "suññāgāra" is at first used to refer to seclusion from worldliness, living in an empty place for practising meditation; and this then leads to its being used symbolically to describe the resulting state of meditation as an emptiness-state. This usage of suñña "empty" (adjective) and suññatā "emptiness" (noun) to refer both to the empty place and to the state of meditation is the first stage in the extension of the common meaning of "emptiness" in early Buddhism.

1.2. The Emptiness of Kong-sanmei/Suññatā-vihāra and Empty World

In early Buddhism, the term "concentrative meditation of emptiness" (kong-sanmei 空三昧[36]) or "abode (state)[37] of emptiness" (suññatā-vihāra) denotes highly valued meditative attainment, whereas "empty world" (suñña-loka) is based on the relationship between the teaching of not-self and emptiness.

Firstly, concerning the concentrative meditation of emptiness/the abode (state) of emptiness, SA 236 says:[38]

> The Buddha asked Śāriputra: "Into which meditative abode (meditative state, chanzhu 禪住) do you enter at this time [in the forest]?"
>
> Śāriputra answered the Buddha: "World-Honoured One, at this time in the forest I enter the meditative abode of the **concentrative meditation of emptiness** (kong-sanmei 空三昧)."
>
> The Buddha said to Śāriputra: "Good, good, Śāriputra. You are entering the **meditative abode of the elders** (shangzuo-chanzhu 上座禪住[39]) in your seated meditation.

Corresponding to this text is the Pāli Piṇḍapātapārisuddhi-sutta (Discourse on Purity of Almsfood), Majjhima-nikāya, No. 151.[40] It says:

> (The Buddha said:) Sāriputta, your faculties are bright, and your complexion is pure and clear.[41] In which abode (state, vihārena) do you now abide much, Sāriputta?

> (Sāriputta replied:) Venerable Sir, I now abide much in the **abode (state) of emptiness** (suññatā-vihāra).
>
> Good, good, Sāriputta. Surely you, Sāriputta, now abide much in the **abode (state) of great men** (mahāpurisa-vihāra). For this, Sāriputta, is the abode of great men, namely, **emptiness** (suññatā).

The "kong-sanmei" (concentrative meditation of emptiness) in SA 236 corresponds to the "suññatā-vihāra" (abode of emptiness) in MN 151; and the "shangzuo-chanzhu" (meditative abode of the elders) in SA 236 corresponds to the "mahāpurisa-vihāra" (abode of great men) in MN 151. The expressions are different, but the fact that the two versions share in common that this kong-sanmei/suññatā-vihāra is called "the meditative abode of elders/the abode of great men" shows that this "meditative state of emptiness" is a state of wisdom, highly regarded and highly valued among meditations.[42]

Moreover, according to SA 236, Śāriputra's kong-sanmei (concentrative meditation of emptiness) is attained in seated meditation, but the Buddha tells Śāriputra that if a monk wishes to abide in the shangzuo-chanzhu (meditative abode of the elders), he should practise awareness of, and fading away of craving, of longing, and of impure attachment when he is going for almsfood, receiving almsfood, or leaving after walking for almsfood, and during the night and day (indicating everyday life in walking, standing, sitting, and reclining).[43] For "craving, longing, and impure attachment" MN 151 has "desire (rāga), hatred (dosa), delusion (moha)[44], and sensory reaction (paṭigha)".[45] Either way, these could be covered by "craving" (taṇhā) or by "desire, hatred, and delusion", because craving is the origin of suffering,[46] and the extinction of craving, or the extinction of desire, hatred, and delusion, is the definition of nirvana (nibbāna).[47] Thus, kong-sanmei or suññatā-vihāra is a meditative state that is empty of craving or of desire, hatred, and delusion in everyday life, not only in seated meditation; and "emptiness" (suññatā) here has the meaning of "absence of craving", or "absence of desire, hatred, and delusion".

Next, "emptiness" also has the meaning of "not-self" in the teaching of "empty world" (suñña-loka). For example, a verse in Sutta-nipāta, Pārāyaṇa-vagga, reads as follows:

> O Mogharaja, always being mindful, removing the view of self (attānudiṭṭhiṃ ūhacca), see the world as empty (suññato lokaṃ avekkhassu), so you may overcome death. The king of death will not see the one who thus sees the world.[48]

This indicates that there is a close relationship between "removing the view of self" and "seeing the world as empty": seeing the emptiness of the world is based on seeing not-self (anatta). Concerning the "world as empty", the Buddha had the following conversation with Ānanda, recorded at SN 35. 85.[49] Ānanda asks:

> Venerable Sir, it is said "the world is empty! the world is empty! (suñño loko)" But in what regard, venerable Sir, is it said that the world is empty?

The Buddha answers:

> Ānanda, it is said that the world is empty because the world is empty of self or of anything belonging to self (suññam attena vā attaniyena vā).

> And what, Ānanda, is empty of self or of anything belonging to self?

> Ānanda, eye is empty of self or of anything belonging to self (cakkhuṃ suññaṃ attena vā attaniyena vā). Material forms (rūpā) are empty of self or of anything belonging to self. Visual consciousness (cakkhu-viññāṇaṃ) is empty of self or of anything belonging to self. Visual contact (cakkhusamphasso) is empty of self or of anything belonging to self. And the rest ... (ear, nose, tongue, body, mind) are empty of self or of anything belonging to self. Also, whatever feeling (vedayitaṃ) pleasant or unpleasant or neither-pleasant-nor-unpleasant arises conditioned by mind-contact (manosamphassa-paccayā) is empty of self or of anything belonging to self.

Corresponding to this text in the Chinese is SA 232,[50] though here the Buddha is conversing with Samṛddhi (P. Samiddhi). According to SA 232, when Samṛddhi asks the same question, the Buddha replies:

> Eye is empty (眼空 Skt. cakṣuḥ śūnyam), empty of eternal and unchanging nature (常恆不變易法空 Skt. śāśvatenāvipariṇāmadharmeṇa śūnyam), empty of anything belonging to self (我所空 Skt. ātmīyena śūnyam). Why is this so? This is nature as it is (此性自爾 Skt. prakṛtir asyaiṣā). Material forms, visual consciousness, visual contact, the feelings unpleasant or pleasant or neither-unpleasant-nor-pleasant that arise conditioned by visual contact are empty, empty of eternal and unchanging nature, empty of anything belonging to self. Why is this so? This is nature as it is. Ear, nose, tongue, body and mind are also thus. This is called "empty world" (空世間 Skt. śūnyo loko).

Although the two texts use slightly different expressions - e.g. "empty of eternal and unchanging nature" (常恆不變

易法空) and "this is nature as it is" (此性自爾) are lacking in SN 35. 85 - the meaning of "empty world" is the same in both.

Accordingly, the Buddha in the SN and SA versions refers to *the six sense-spheres* (saḷāyatana; including *the six sense-faculties*[51] and *the six types of external object*[52]), *six consciousnesses,*[53] *six contacts,*[54] and *six feelings*[55] as "the world" (loka). Also, he focuses on the "sentient being" (P. satta, Skt. sattva) when looking at the world.[56] *The six sense-faculties* corresponding to *the six types of external object* produce *the six types of consciousness.* The coming together of these three phenomena (i.e. the six sense-faculties, the six external objects, and the six types of consciousness) is *the six contacts.* Through *the six contacts, the six feelings* are produced,[57] each of which is either pleasant feeling, unpleasant feeling, or neither-pleasant-nor-unpleasant feeling (i.e. neutral feeling).[58] These inter-relationships or inter-connections in the view of the world can be shown as follows:

sense-faculties	**external objects**	**consciousness, etc.**
eye -------------------	visible forms -------	visual cons., etc.
ear --------------------	sounds --------------	auditory cons., etc.
nose ------------------	odours --------------	olfactory cons., etc.
tongue --------------	tastes ---------------	gustatory cons., etc.
body ----------------	tangible things -----	tactile cons., etc.
mind (manas) -------	mind-objects -------	mental cons., etc.

As shown above, the two versions record in common that every one of these – the six sense-spheres (six sense-faculties and six external objects), six types of consciousness, contact, and feeling – is empty of self or of anything belonging to self. Since these are not-self, the world is empty of self. Thus, the notion of "not-self" in the two traditions is the basis for saying "the world is empty"; here "emptiness" has the meaning of "not-self".

It is important to note here that in explaining the meaning of the world as empty, the Buddha in the discourses does not say that eye itself (etc.) is *empty*. He says "eye is *empty of self* (suññaṃ attena) or *of anything belonging to self*" (attaniyena). It is not that the eye itself, or any of the other items is *empty*.

To summarise this section, two uses and meanings of "emptiness" have been noted: (1) In the teaching of 空三昧 kong-sanmei/suññatā-vihāra "emptiness" means "empty of craving or of desire, hatred, and delusion". The meditative state of emptiness (kong-sanmei/suññatā-vihāra) is a state of wisdom, highly valued among meditations. Also this is the *ultimate meaning of emptiness* in early Buddhism, since it is connected with the meaning of nirvana (nibbāna). (2) In the teaching of suñña-loka "empty world", "emptiness" means "not-self". The notion of not-self is "A is empty of B, but A is not empty." Also this is a *basic meaning of emptiness* in early Buddhism, because seeing the world as empty is the key to bringing about the fading away of craving or of desire, hatred, and delusion. To see the world as empty is to get rid of the self-view, and the self-view is the root cause of craving (or desire, hatred, and delusion). (How to see the world as empty of self in early Buddhism will be discussed in 1.4. "The Recognition of Emptiness".)

1.3. Conditioned Genesis, Nirvana and Emptiness

Conditioned genesis (P. paṭiccasamuppāda, Skt. pratītyasamutpāda) is a fundamental principle of the Buddha's teaching. Insight into conditioned genesis leads to "nirvana" (P. nibbāna, Skt. nirvāṇa); and, as will be shown below, both conditioned genesis and nirvana are connected with emptiness.

Firstly, we discuss conditioned genesis as a principle of the Buddha's teaching. According to SN 12, 65[59] and SA 287,[60] the Buddha discovered and realised the dharma (the nature of phenomena) of conditioned genesis in meditation as he attained enlightenment (sambodha); and he declared, revealed, and taught the dharma leading to nirvana for humankind. "Conditioned genesis" refers to this principle: "When this exists, that exists; this arising, that arises. When this does not exist, that does not exist; this ceasing, that ceases." (imasmiṃ sati idaṃ hoti, imassuppādā idaṃ uppajjati. imasmiṃ asati idaṃ na hoti, imassa nirodhā idaṃ nirujjhati).[61] The reference is particularly to the origin of suffering (dukkha) and the cessation of suffering (i.e. nibbāna, nirvāṇa). The Buddha refers to the means for realizing this principle as "the ancient way of the noble (enlightened) ones". It is his noble eightfold way, the way leading to knowledge of the four noble truths, or of conditioned genesis. According to both texts (SN 12 65 and SA 287), after having discovered and fully realised the dharma of conditioned genesis in his meditation, the Buddha says:

> ... thus I have attained to the ancient way of the noble (enlightened) ones: ... right view, right aim, right speech, right action, right livelihood, right effort, right mindfulness, right concentrative meditation. . . . I have gone along this path and seen *aging-and-death,*[62] *the origin of aging-and-death,*[63] *the ceasing of aging-and-death,*[64] *the path leading to the ceasing of aging-and-death.*[65] In the same way, I have fully come to know birth ..., becoming ..., attachment ..., craving ..., feeling ..., contact ..., the six sense-spheres ..., name-and-material form ..., consciousness ..., *activities, the origin of activities, the ceasing of activities, the path leading to the ceasing of activities.*

The representative formulation of conditioned genesis lists twelve factors. In the forward order - the origin of suffering: when this exists, that exists - these twelve factors are as follows:

(1) Conditioned by *ignorance* (avijjā), activities (saṃkhārā) arise (or exist);
(2) conditioned by *activities*, consciousness (viññāṇa) arises;
(3) conditioned by *consciousness*, name-and-material form (nāma-rūpa)[66] arise;
(4) conditioned by *name-and-material form*, the six sense-spheres (saḷāyatana) arise;
(5) conditioned by *the six sense-spheres*, contact (phassa) arises;
(6) conditioned by *contact*, feeling (vedanā) arises;
(7) conditioned by *feeling*, craving (taṇhā) arises;
(8) conditioned by *craving*, attachment (upādāna) arises;
(9) conditioned by *attachment*, becoming (bhava) arises;
(10) conditioned by *becoming*, birth (jāti) arises;
(11) conditioned by *birth* arise
(12) *aging-and-death, along with grief, lamentation, pain, depression and despair* (jarā-maraṇa-soka-parideva-dukkha-domanassa-upāyāsa); thus arises (exists) this whole mass of suffering.

In negative formulation - the cessation of suffering: when this does not exist, that does not exist - the twelve factors are: Conditioned by the ceasing of ignorance, activities cease; conditioned by the ceasing of activities, consciousness ceases; ... thus ceases this whole mass of suffering.

While this is the representative formulation, conditioned genesis does not always have twelve factors in early Buddhist texts. There also exist accounts of it which list five factors,[67] eight,[68] nine,[69] ten,[70] or eleven factors,[71] as well as the usual twelve factors. The statement of conditioned genesis with just five factors runs: (1) craving, (2) attachment, (3) becoming, (4) birth, and (5) "aging-and-death, along with grief, lamentation, pain, depression and despair." This most concise formula corresponds directly to two of the four noble truths, since (5) "aging-and-death, along with grief, lamentation, pain, depression and despair" is suffering (first truth), and (1) craving (taṇhā) is the origin of suffering (second truth). Since craving is itself a conditioned phenomenon, the series of causes can be extended to as many as twelve factors.

At SN 12, 20[72] and its Chinese counterpart SA 296,[73] and also at SA 299,[74] it is stated that conditioned genesis is not something made by the Buddha himself or by others: whether or not a Buddha arises in the world, this is the status of dharma (P. dhammaṭṭhitatā, 法住 Skt. dharma-sthititā), the certainty of dharma (P. dhamma-niyāmatā, 法定 Skt. dharma-niyāmatā), the fact of causal connection (P. idappaccayatā) – or the element (nature) of dharma (法界 Skt. dharma-dhātu). In other words, the texts in the Pāli and Chinese versions record in common that conditioned genesis is a principle of nature, of phenomena as they really are.

This principle is connected with emptiness. At SN 20 7, the Buddha says:

> Those discourses uttered by the Tathāgata (the Buddha) are profound, deep in meaning, supramundane (lokuttarā), **connected with emptiness** (suññata-paṭisaṃyuttā).[75]

By "discourses (suttanta)" is meant the teaching or dharma of the Buddha. That teaching is profound, deep in meaning, because it is supramundane and connected with emptiness. The teaching of the Buddha is profound, deep in meaning because it is connected with the emptiness of the supramundane.

As shown above, the Buddha used conditioned genesis as the basis for teaching dharma (the nature of phenomena), which leads to nirvana (the cessation of suffering), so the dharma of conditioned genesis is also profound. Thus, there are two profound dharmas connected with emptiness: conditioned genesis and nirvana. At SN 6. 1, the Buddha says:

> I have penetrated this dharma that is profound, difficult to see, hard to understand, peaceful, excellent, beyond the sphere of thought, subtle, realisable only by the wise. ... namely causal connection: **conditioned genesis** (idappaccayatā: paṭiccasamuppādo). This too is difficult to see, namely the calming of all activities, the renunciation of all defilements, the extinction of craving, detachment, cessation: **nirvana** (sabba-saṅkhārasamatho sabbupadhi-paṭinissaggo taṇha-kkhayo virāgo nirodho: nibbānaṃ).[76]

Similarly at SA 293 he says:

> I teach to monks this Dharma: the noble, the supramundane, **connected with emptiness**, according to the dharma of conditioned genesis[77]. ... Profound is this, namely **conditioned genesis**; even more profound, more difficult to see is this, namely the renunciation of all attachments, the extinction of craving, fading away of desire, cessation: **nirvana**.[78] These two dharmas are namely the **compounded** (有爲 Skt. saṃskṛta, P. saṃkhata, i.e. conditioned genesis) and the **uncompounded** (無爲 Skt. asaṃskṛta, P. asaṃkhata, i.e. nirvana). The com-

> pounded is arising, persisting, changing, passing away. The uncompounded is not arising, not persisting, not changing, not passing away.[79]

As stated in section 1.2, in the term "kong-sanmei" 空三昧 (concentrative meditation of emptiness) or "suññatā-vihāra" (abode of emptiness) "emptiness" has the meaning of "absence of craving (taṇhā) or of desire (rāga), hatred (dosa), and delusion (moha)"; and in the term "suñña-loka" (empty world) "emptiness" has the meaning of "not-self". These two meanings of "emptiness" relate to the cycle of birth and death (saṃsāra)[80] or to the world (loka).[81] However, the complete cessation of craving or of desire, hatred, and delusion manifests the emptiness of the supramundane, nirvana: the *asaṃkhata* (uncompounded, unconditioned, absolute). The definition of "nirvana" is: "the extinction of craving" (taṇhakkhayo),[82] and this is identical with the definition of "asaṃkhata": "the extinction of desire, the extinction of hatred, the extinction of delusion" (rāgakkhayo dosakkhayo mohakkhayo).[83] Thus, of the above two meanings of emptiness, "not-self" is of key significance for the vision of "empty world", but "the complete extinction of craving"[84] is of ultimate significance because of its connection with "the uncompounded", nirvana.

"Emptiness" applies to nirvana, the uncompounded, the supramundane, because the supramundane is empty of craving. "Emptiness" also applies to conditioned genesis, the compounded world (loka): the compounded world is empty of self ("empty world" suñña-loka), and seeing this one can develop the emptiness which consists in the extinction of all afflictions (kilesa) and of all suffering (dukkha); one can attain nirvana.

Conditioned genesis is profound, deep in meaning, because of the connection with emptiness, the profundity of nirvana, by this principle: "When this exists, that exists; this arising, that arises" – indicating the origin of suffering: the world (loka); "when this does not exist, that does not exist; this ceasing, that ceases" – indicating the cessation of suffering: nirvana.

Therefore, **emptiness** is based on **conditioned genesis** to link with the compounded: the world (loka), the cycle of birth and death (saṃsāra), and with the uncompounded: **nirvana**. Thus, conditioned genesis is a principle of both the compounded and the uncompounded.

1.4. The Recognition of Emptiness

As stated in 1.3, the discourses in the Pāli and Chinese versions record that the Buddha used conditioned genesis to point the way to nirvana, and stated that both conditioned genesis and nirvana are profound, connected with emptiness. The two versions also show he indicated that one should first realise the dharma (the nature of phenomena) of conditioned genesis, and then one will come to have the wisdom of nirvana. For example, at SN 12. 70 and SA 347 he says:

> Susīma, first [one comes to have] *knowledge of dharma-status* (the nature of phenomena), afterwards [one comes to have] *knowledge of nirvana*. (pubbe kho Susīma dhammaṭṭhitiññāṇaṃ pacchā nibbāne ñāṇanti).[85]

"Knowledge of dharma-status" (P. dhamma-ṭhiti-ñāṇa, Skt. dharma-sthiti-jñāna) refers to knowledge of the dharma of conditioned genesis.[86] According to both the Pāli and the Chinese texts (SN 12. 70 and SA 347), a person who attains this "knowledge of dharma-status" is called "one who is wisdom-liberated" (P. paññā-vimutta, Skt. prajñā-vimukta), so a person who attains "knowledge of nirvana" (P. nibbāna-ñāṇa, Skt. nirvāṇa-jñāna), which comes after having the "knowledge of dharma-status", is called "one who has twofold-liberation" (P. ubhatobhāga-vimutta, Skt. Ubhayato-bhāga-vimukta).[87] Both "wisdom liberation" (P. paññā-vimutti, Skt. prajñā-vimukti) and "twofold liberation" (P. ubhatobhāga-vimutti, Skt. ubhayatobhāga-vimukti) entail first knowing the dharma of conditioned genesis, and then knowing the dharma of nirvana.

Consequently, realising the dharma of conditioned genesis is a first step to comprehending the profound dharmas of conditioned genesis and nirvana, which are empty; however, since there are various levels on which to understand the "emptiness" of conditioned genesis in early Buddhist texts, to observe the meaning of emptiness it is necessary to look at it both from the viewpoint of impermanence (P. anicca, Skt. anitya), and from the viewpoint of the middle path (P. majjhimā paṭipadā, Skt. madhyamā pratipadā). In other words, conditioned genesis is connected with emptiness by virtue of both "impermanence" and the "middle way".

1.4.A. Emptiness from the Viewpoint of Conditioned Genesis as Impermanence

The Buddha's path to liberation (vimutti) begins with recognising suffering in the nature of life. In terms of the "four noble truths" (cattāri ariyasaccāni)[88] one must achieve full knowing (pariññeyya[89]):

(1) knowledge (pariññā) of suffering (dukkha),
(2) elimination (pahāna) of the arising of suffering (dukkha-samudaya[90]),

(3) attainment (sacchikiriyā) of the cessation of suffering (dukkha-nirodha[91]) and,
(4) development (bhāvanā) of the way leading to the cessation of suffering (dukkha-nirodha-gāminī-paṭipadā[92]).

These four noble truths apply an easier way of comprehending the principle of conditioned genesis to show how suffering arises, and how it can be made to cease; but it is easy to overlook the fact that suffering ("the world") and nirvana (the supramundane) are based on the same principle. Seeing the nature of phenomena, developing the wisdom (paññā) that is connected with the ending of suffering or with mind free from "affliction-flow" (anāsavacittassa), is identified as noble, supramundane "right view" (sammādiṭṭhi);[93] and this right view is said to be the leader or forerunner (pubbaṅgama) on the way to the cessation of suffering, to liberation.[94]

Consequently, how to see and know compounded nature as suffering is a significant observation in Buddhist thinking. Conditioned genesis indicates that all compounded things are impermanent (anicca), and because they are impermanent they are also suffering. For example, at SN 12. 20, following an explanation of conditioned genesis, the Buddha says:

> And what, monks, is the dharma of "arisen by condition" (paṭiccasamuppanna)? Aging-and-death (and birth, becoming, attachment, craving, feeling, contact, the six sense-spheres, name-and-material form, consciousness, activities, ignorance) are **impermanent** (aniccaṃ), compounded things (or conditioned things, saṅkhataṃ), arisen by condition (paṭiccasamuppannaṃ), have perishable nature, (khayadhammaṃ), the nature of decay (vayadham-

> maṃ), fading way (virāgadhammaṃ), cessation (nirodha-dhammaṃ).[95]

Hence, conditioned genesis indicates that compounded things "arisen by condition" are impermanent, and so have perishable nature, the nature of decay, fading away, and cessation.

The notion that "that which is impermanent is suffering" can be seen in many texts of both the Pāli Saṃyutta-nikāya and the Chinese Saṃyuktāgama. For example, SN 36. 11 and its counterpart SA 474 state there are three kinds of feeling,[96] but "whatsoever is felt is within suffering" (yaṃ kiñci vedayitaṃ taṃ dukkhasmin). The reason that whatsoever feeling a person experiences is within suffering is stated by the Buddha at SN 36. 11:

> ... Monk! Concerning (sandhāya) the impermanence of compounded things (saṅkhārānaṃ yeve anicca-taṃ), I have said that whatsoever is felt is within suffering. Monk! Concerning the perishable nature (khayadhammataṃ) of compounded things, their nature of decaying (vayadhammataṃ), fading way (virāgadhammataṃ), ceasing (nirodhadhammataṃ), changing for the worse (vipariṇāmadhammataṃ), I have said that whatsoever is felt is within suffering.[97]

The corresponding SA 474 states:

> The Buddha said to Ānanda: Because all compounded things (行 Skt. saṃskārāḥ) are impermanent (無常 Skt. anitya), all compounded things are changing by nature (變易法), I have said all feelings are suffering (諸所有受悉皆是苦). Also Ānanda, because of the gradual cessation of compounded things, the gradual calming of

> compounded things, I have said all feelings are suffering.[98]

Thus, although the two versions differ in wording, they share a common view that compounded things are impermanent (anicca); therefore, all feelings are suffering (dukkha).

This teaching of suffering is stated from the viewpoint of the "impermanence" of compounded nature: one must see that impermanence is suffering in the nature of life. In other words, to know suffering in the nature of life is also to know that the "five aggregates",[99] "six sense-spheres",[100] or "eighteen elements"[101] of conditioned genesis (compounded nature) are impermanent, and that is the suffering of aging, death, sorrow, distress, depression, and affliction. These are the reality of the body and mind of sentient beings. The connection between impermanence and suffering is particularly in the sense that sentient beings unawares and unconsciously attach to the impermanent nature of compounded things as mentally projecting a permanent entity (absolute substance) belonging to "my self"; therefore, when the compounded phenomena of attachment change or become different constantly, the suffering of grief, lamentation, pain, depression, and despair comes to exist.[102] In other words, impermanence is suffering when one attaches to (whether within or beyond) the compounded phenomena as a self (entity) or as belonging to my self. This teaching of why impermanence is suffering to sentient beings is common to the Pāli and the Chinese versions of early Buddhist canon.

Consequently, there is no question that impermanence is suffering in early Buddhist thinking, since there are many statements in early Buddhist texts that "impermanence is suffering".

What concerns us here is how impermanence (and therefore suffering) is connected with emptiness. As noted above, in early Buddhism "emptiness" has not-self as its main meaning, and nirvana as its ultimate meaning. Thus, the relationship between impermanence and emptiness is as stated at SA 270:

> One who practises the perception of impermanence (anicca-saññā) can establish the perception of not-self (anatta-saññā). The mind of a noble disciple who abides in the perception of not-self is aloof from self-pride (asmi-māna), and will go on to nirvana. (無常想者，能建立無我想，聖弟子住無我想，心離我慢，順得涅槃。)[103]

The corresponding Pāli text, SN 22. 102, says:

> Thus developed and practised, monks, the perception of impermanence (aniccasaññā), exhausts all desire for sensuality (kāmarāgam), exhausts all desire for material form (rūparāgam), exhausts all desire for becoming (bhavarāgam), exhausts all ignorance (avijjam), removes all self-pride (asmimānaṃ). (Evam bhāvitā kho bhikkhave aniccasaññā evam bahulīkatā, sabbaṃ kāmarāgam pariyādiyati, sabbaṃ rūparāgam pariyādiyati, sabbam bhavarāgam pariyādiyati, sabbam avijjam pariyādiyati, sabbam asmimānaṃ samūhantīti)[104]

Similarly, another Pāli discourse, AN 9. 3 states:

> Meghiya, the one who thinks on impermanence establishes the perception of not-self; thinking on not-self, uprooting self-pride, he attains nirvana in this very life. (Aniccasaññino Meghiya anattasaññā

> saṇṭhāti, anattasaññī asmimānasamugghātaṃ pāpuṇāti diṭṭh' eva dhamme nibbānan ti)[105]

Hence, both the Chinese and the Pāli versions record in common that there is a close relationship between the thought of impermanence and the understanding of not-self (removing self-pride) and nirvana.

Self-pride (asmi-māna[106]) is pride that attaches to "I am"; it is egotism. Its removal is based on the insight of not-self (anatta). The exhausting of all desire for sensuality, material form, and becoming, and of all ignorance is the wisdom of liberation (vimutti). Seeing (passati) the nature of things as "impermanent" (= suffering) leads to removal of the view of self, and so to the realisation of nirvana. This is, then, for early Buddhism, a major way of "insight" (vipassanā)[107] leading to liberation. Insight into the compounded nature of the "five aggregates" or the "six sense-spheres" as impermanent is therefore called "right view" (sammādiṭṭhi) in early Buddhism.[108] And to see that "compounded nature is impermanent, what is impermanent is suffering, what is suffering is not-self" is also regarded as "right insight" or "right wisdom" (sammappaññā).[109]

There are, in early Buddhist texts, two formulations of these characteristics to be observed in compounded things:

(1) impermanent (anicca), suffering (dukkha), not-self (anatta).
(2) impermanent, suffering, empty (suñña), not-self.

The first formulation is most common in both the Chinese *Saṃyuktāgama* and the Pāli *Saṃyutta-nikāya*. The two versions contain frequent references to the attainment of liberation or nirvana through insight into the "five aggregates" or the "six sense-spheres" as "impermanent, suffering, and not-self".[110]

"Not-self" is also expressed as "not-belonging-to-self" (anattaniya) or "not-self-and-not-belonging-to-self" (anattan-anattaniya).[111] It is also defined in the Pāli Saṃyutta-nikāya as "this is not mine, I am not this, this is not my self" (n'etam mama, neso 'ham asmi, na m'eso attā).[112] The counterpart of this three-phrase expression in the Chinese Saṃyuktāgama is: "this is not self, this is not other than self, neither is self in this nor this in self" (非我, 不異我, 不相在).[113] The set of three phrases – "this is not mine, I am not this, this is not my self" or "this is not self, this is not other than self, neither is self in this nor this in self" – is frequently seen in the two versions.[114] Thus, comparing the two traditions, it is clear that this three-phrase expression in early Buddhist texts has the same meaning as "not-self-and-not-belonging-to-self", "not-belonging-to-self", or just "not-self"; "impermanent, suffering, not-self" can be used as a set of principles for observing compounded nature.

The southern tradition (Pāli Buddhism) emphasises only "impermanent, suffering, and not-self", whereas the northern tradition prefers the second formulation with four terms, "impermanence, suffering, emptiness, not-self". This is evident from the fact that the four terms are frequently found together as a set in the Chinese texts,[115] but are not found together in the Pāli except in conjunction with other terms, as discussed below.

The four terms do sometimes occur in corresponding Chinese and Pāli texts. For example, SA 259 states that the five aggregates should be seen thus:

> ... as sickness, as swelling, as arrow, as pain; as **impermanence**, as **suffering**, as **emptiness**, as **not-self** (wuchang 無常, ku 苦, kong 空, wuwo 無我).[116]

And the corresponding Pāli, SN 22. 122, says they should be seen thus:

> ... as **impermanence**, as **suffering**, as sickness, as swelling, as arrow, as pain, as illness, as alien, as decay, as **emptiness**, as **not-self** ... (... aniccato dukkhato ... suññato anattato ...)[117]

In both versions the basic set of four terms "impermanence, suffering, emptiness, not-self" is accompanied by extra words – four in the Chinese, seven in the Pāli – which graphically indicate the concreteness of suffering. The extra terms are also differently placed in the two texts; however, "emptiness" is clearly part of the standard set: "impermanence, suffering, emptiness, not-self".

Thus, the two formulations listed above, whether of three terms or four, are found in both traditions in teachings relating to "insight".

Here it is necessary to examine the inclusion of "emptiness" in the four-term set: "impermanence, suffering, emptiness, not-self". Do these different formulations represent significant differences in meaning? What is the significance of the word-order, with emptiness preceding not-self? And do "emptiness" and "not-self" really have the same meaning or not?

In this connection, the EA version states that "impermanence is suffering; suffering is not-self; not-self is emptiness;"[118] "emptiness is this-is-not-my-self/this-is-not-mine, self-is-not-in-this/I-am-not-this,"[119] or "emptiness is neither-existence-nor-non-existence, meaning also not-self."[120] Thus, the sequence of the four-term set in the EA tradition is: "impermanence, suffering, not-self, emptiness"; "not-self" comes before "emptiness", and "emptiness" is mainly defined as "not-self" (referring also "this-is-not-my-self, self-is-not-in-this," "neither-existence-nor-non-existence").

Also, as noted above, "not-self" or "not-belonging-to-self" is a key meaning of "emptiness", while "nirvana" is its ultimate meaning. In early Buddhism, to see the nature of compounded things is to see "what is impermanent is suffering, and what is suffering is not-self." "Impermanence, suffering, not-self" is the basic way, perhaps the only way, of insight leading to nirvana. It follows that the adding of "emptiness" alongside "not-self", to yield the four-term set, is based on the narrow or basic meaning of "emptiness", not on the ultimate meaning. Emptiness here means only "not-self" and "not-belonging-to-self" or it means the three-phrase set: "this is not mine, I am not this, this is not my self" / "this is not self, this is not other than self, neither is self in this nor this in self". Therefore, the four-term expression, with "emptiness" preceding "not-self", says no more than the three-term expression. The meaning is simply: "impermanence, suffering, not-self".

In conclusion, to realise "emptiness" by seeing the nature of compounded things – the "five aggregates", the "six sense-spheres", etc. – as "impermanent" focuses on understanding of "suffering" in the nature of life that is not permanently or absolutely self. This leads to aloofness from "suffering" by destruction of self-attachment (craving), and then to nirvana – the ending of suffering – by the ceasing of self-attachment. Thus, "impermanence" is an important notion for understanding the meaning of emptiness in early Buddhism.

1.4.B. Emptiness from the Viewpoint of Conditioned Genesis as the Middle Way

Conditioned genesis is called "the middle way" (majjhimā paṭipadā) by the Buddha because it avoids extreme views, which are mainly based on self-view (atta-diṭṭhi). Insight into conditioned genesis as the middle way is identified with "right view", and with nirvana. This is made clear at SN 12. 15:

> (The venerable Kaccāyana asked the Buddha:) Venerable Sir, it is said: 'right view, right view' (sammādiṭṭhi). From what aspect it is said 'right view', venerable Sir?
>
> (The Buddha replied:) This world, Kaccāyana, usually depends on two [extremes] (dvaya-nissito): existence (atthitā) and non-existence (natthitā).
>
> Now, Kaccāyana, one who with right wisdom (sammappaññāya) sees (passato) the arising of the world (lokasamudayaṃ) as it really is (yathā-bhūtaṃ) does not hold to the non-existence of the world (loke natthitā). One who with right wisdom sees the ceasing of the world (lokanirodhaṃ) as it really is does not hold to the existence of the world (loke atthitā).
>
> Kaccāyana, this world is usually approaching attachment, tending towards bondage (upāyupādānābhini-vesavinibandho). And one whose mind does not come to approaching attachment, obstinacy, tending towards bias (upāyupādānām cetaso adhiṭṭhānam abhinivesānusayaṃ no upeti) does not cling to, does

> not insist on, not [attaching to] "it is my self" (na upādiyati nādhiṭṭhāti attā na me ti).[121] Then, when suffering arises, it arises; when suffering ceases, it ceases (dukkham eva uppajjamānam uppajjati dukkhaṃ nirujjhamānaṃ nirujjhatīti). One is not in doubt, is not perplexed (na kaṅkhati na vicikicchati). Here, one who is not dependent on others comes to have knowledge/insight (aparapaccayā ñāṇam evassa ettha hoti). Thus this, Kaccāyana, is 'right view'.
>
> Kaccāyana, 'Everything exists' (sabbam atthīti), this is one extreme (eko anto). 'Everything does not exist' (sabbaṃ natthīti), this the other extreme (dutiyo anto). Kaccāyana, not approaching the two extremes (ubho ante anupagamma), the Tathāgata (the Buddha) teaches you the Dharma by *the middle* [*way*] (majjhena):
>
> Conditioned by ignorance are activities; conditioned by activities is consciousness, and so forth. Thus arises this whole mass of suffering. But by the total fading away and ceasing of ignorance activities ceases; from the ceasing of activities, consciousness ceases, and so forth. Thus ceases this whole mass of suffering.[122]

The content of this Pāli text is almost the same as that of SA 301.[123] The notion of "neither existence nor non-existence" has the same meaning as nirvana. That is, as noted in 1.3, nirvana is unconditioned and uncompounded, neither arising nor ceasing. Also, according to SA 249, nirvana is not existence (you-yu 有 餘 = remainder), not non-existence (wu-yu 無 餘 = no remainder), not both-existence-and-non-existence, and not neither-existence-nor-non-existence.[124] This insight into conditioned genesis as the middle way does not imply attachment to the middle ground, nor does it mean being unsure about which side is right. It means to be devoid (empty) of the two extremes: the self-based view of existence and the self-based view of non-existence. And it directly implies the meaning of nirvana. In other words, "the middle way of conditioned genesis" has the same meaning as "the emptiness of nirvana".

Clearly, this approach to insight is very different from that which focuses on "impermanence (= suffering)" to eliminate self-view and thus lead to nirvana. The way of right view consisting in seeing conditioned genesis as the middle way, involves directly seeing that there is, in the nature of phenomena, neither existence nor non-existence, so as to see directly the emptiness or not-self-hood of phenomena and thus attain nirvana.

Concerning this middle way of conditioned genesis, there is raised a question linking impermanence, not-self and nirvana. According to SN 22. 90 and SA 262,[125] a bhikkhu ("monk") Chanda (P. Channa), who has not yet achieved the wisdom of nirvana, asks various other bhikkhus to teach him dharma (P. dhamma). They teach him that material form (rūpa), feeling (vedanā), perception (saññā), activities (saṃkhārā) and consciousness (viññāṇa) are impermanent (anicca) and, as compounded things, are not self (anatta).[126] Chanda replies: I do know that material form, feeling, perception, activities and consciousness are impermanent, and being compounded things, are not self.[127] Nevertheless, I (Chanda) do not understand and delight when I hear of "the *calming* of all activities, renunciation of all attachment, the destruction of craving, the fading away of desire, cessation: **nirvana**." (sabbasaṅkhārasamathe sabbhūpadhi-paṭinissagge taṇhakkhaye virāge nirodhe nibbāne). For the section in quote marks the Chinese SA 262 has: "the *emptiness* of all activities, renunciation of attachment, the destruction of craving, the fading away of desire: **nirvana**." (一切諸行空寂，不可得，愛盡，離欲，涅槃). Thus where the Pāli has "calming" (samatha), the Chinese has "emptiness" (空寂).

Chanda's point is that all activities (compounded things, saṅkhārā) are impermanent and not-self; but nirvana is not characterised by impermanence and not-self, and thus there is something, some metaphysical entity, for oneself to attain in the cessation of nirvana (the ending of suffering). If there is complete emptiness in nirvana, who then is the self? or, what is meant by the self seeing (passati) the dharma (the nature of phenomena)? That is, the dharma of compounded nature (saṅkhata) and uncompounded nature (asaṅkhata) are divided into two different things. Chanda admitted impermanence and not-self of compounded nature (saṅkhata-dhamma) as essential for the ending of suffering; but he could not admit the uncompounded nature (asaṅkhata-dhamma) of nirvana where all activities are empty (or "calm") of self.

Harbouring this doubt, Chanda goes to ask the venerable Ānanda. Ānanda tells him: "I heard the Buddha teach this to the venerable Kaccāyana:

> This world, Kaccāyana, usually depends on two [extremes]: existence and non-existence ... (the content is as quoted above).

To resolve Chanda's misunderstanding regarding impermanence, not-self, and nirvana, Ānanda helps him to understand compounded nature (saṅkhata = conditioned genesis) as neither existence nor non-existence, and also as the ending of suffering: nirvana. The extreme views of existence and non-existence both come from self-view (atta-diṭṭhi). The extinction of self-view, or of desire, hatred, and delusion, is the uncompounded or unconditioned (asaṃkhata), nirvana itself. That is: "when suffering arises, it arises; when suffering ceases, it ceases"; there is neither arising nor ceasing, and there is neither existence nor non-existence.

To see the arising of the world (loka-samudaya) in terms of the middle way of conditioned genesis is to be aloof from the view of non-existence while not giving rise to the view of existence (eternalism); and to see the ceasing of the world (loka-nirodha) in terms of the middle way of conditioned genesis is to be aloof from the view of existence while not giving rise to the view of non-existence (annihilationism). That is, the middle way of conditioned genesis points to both the arising of the world (existence) and the ceasing of the world (non-existence): the world is of a ceasing-nature, i.e. impermanent, and it is empty of self. Hence, the world (loka), as illusion, is an unreal and an unsolid arising-nature (= ceasing-nature) and is neither existence nor non-existence. If one see this, and gets rid of self view, there is a fading way of the two extreme views, which leads to the emptiness of nirvana.

The early Buddhist texts present other characterisations of "the middle way of conditioned genesis". The following are examples.

(1) The middle way of neither sameness nor difference. SA 297 says:

> Then the Buddha said to the monks: I will teach you the dharma, ... namely: '*the dharma-discourse of great emptiness*' (大空法經 da-kong-fa-jing, Skt. mahāśūnyatā dharmaparyāya) ... For one who has the view which says that *soul* (or life or self, Skt. P. jīva) *is the same thing as body* (Skt. śarīra, P. sarīra), there is no point in the noble life. And for one who has the other view which says that *soul is*

> *one thing and body another*, there is also no point in the noble life. When the mind follows neither of these two extremes, one moves rightly toward the middle way, that is the noble, the supramundane, the true nature of phenomena, free of distortion, having right view, namely: Conditioned by birth are aging-and-death, and similarly conditioned are birth, becoming, attachment, craving, feeling, contact, the six sense-spheres, name-and-form, consciousness, and activities. Conditioned by ignorance, activities arise ... when ignorance ceases, activities cease, and so on ..., and this whole mass of suffering ceases. This is called '*the dharma-discourse of great emptiness*'.[128]

The Pāli counterpart, SN 12. 35-36,[129] has almost the same content, but lacks the words: "the dharma-discourse of great emptiness" (大空法經). However, as noted in 1.2 and 1.3, both traditions have other texts in which the Buddha takes conditioned genesis as the basis for teachings connected with emptiness; and he there describes the meditative state of emptiness (空三昧 kong-sanmei/suññatā-vihāra) as the meditative abode of elders or great men (上座禪住 shangzuo-chanzhu/mahāpurisa-vihāra). Thus the use of the word "great emptiness" in SA 297 to refer to the middle way of conditioned genesis is in keeping with the terminology of early Buddhism.

(2) The middle way of neither eternalism nor annihilationism. At SA 300 the Buddha says:

> To declare that the one who acts is [the same as] the one who experiences [the result] is to fall into the *eternalist view* (P. sassata-diṭṭhi). To declare that one acts and another experiences [the result] is to fall into the *annihilationist view* (P. uccheda-diṭṭhi).

> Teaching the essence, teaching the dharma, I avoid these two extremes. I teach the dharma of the middle way, namely: When this is, that is; this arising, that arises. Conditioned by ignorance, activities arise, ... and thus is the origin of this whole mass of suffering. Ignorance ceasing, activities cease, ... and thus is the ceasing of this whole mass of suffering.[130]

The same discussion of neither eternalism nor annihilationism occurs at SN 12. 17.[131]

(3) The middle way of neither coming nor going. At SA 335 the Buddha says:[132]

> I will teach you dharma, ... namely '*the discourse on emptiness in its ultimate meaning*' (第一義空經 diyiyi-kong-jing, Skt. paramārtha-śūnyatā-sūtra) ... What is the discourse on emptiness in its ultimate meaning? Monks, when the eye arises, *there is no place from which it comes; when it ceases, there is no place to which it goes.* Thus the eye, being not real, arises; having arisen it ceases completely. It is a result of [previous] action (業報 karma/kamma-vipāka) but there is *no doer* (無作者 Skt. akartṛka = no self); when these aggregates (Skt. skandhāḥ) cease, other aggregates continue, except in *conventional dharma* (俗數法 sushu-fa, Skt. Dharma-saṃketa). The same teachings apply also to the ear, nose, tongue, body, and mind, except in conventional dharma. The meaning of conventional dharma is: Because this exists, that exists; because this arises, that arises, thus: Conditioned by ignorance are activities; conditioned by activities is consciousness, and so on ... and thus arises this whole mass of suffering. And again, when this does not exist, that

> does not exist; when this ceases, that ceases. When ignorance ceases, activities cease; when activities cease, consciousness ceases, and so on ... and thus ceases this whole mass of suffering. Monks, this is called '*the discourse on emptiness in its ultimate meaning*'.[133]

Similarly, at SA 273 the Buddha says:

> ... Monk, just as two hands coming together produce sound, so conditioned by eye and [visible] forms, is produced visual consciousness, and these three things together produce contact. [Conditioned by] Contact arise feeling, perception, and activities. All these dharmas (phenomena) are not-self and impermanent. This impermanent self is not eternal, not stable, a changing self. Why is this so? Monk, this is the dharma (nature) of birth, aging, death, and rebirth. Monk, all compounded things (Skt. saṃskārāḥ, P. saṅkhārā) are as an illusion, a flame, ceasing in an instant, *not really coming* (or *arising*), *not really going* (or *ceasing*). Therefore, monk, you should know, rejoice in and be mindful of this: all activities are empty; empty of permanent, eternal status, unchanging nature; not-self-and-not-belonging-to-self.[134]

These two texts (SA 335 and 273), both of which lack Pāli counterpart, describe the six sense-spheres as of conditioned nature and empty of self, and thus as empty of either coming or going.

In SA 335, the "conventional dharma" (俗數法 sushu-fa) refers to conditioned genesis, and the not-self of neither coming nor going together with the dharma of conditioned genesis is called "emptiness in its ultimate meaning" (第一義空 diyiyi-kong, Skt. paramārtha-śūnyatā).

In my view, these two texts indicate that the cause and the effect of conditioned nature in each arising and disappearing (ceasing) moment reveal the nature (dharma) of *the passage of time*. These cause and effect in *time* are neither the same nor different, and nothing remains constant for even a single moment in the series of causes and effects.

(4) The middle way of the fourteen "non-declarations" (P. avyākata, Skt. avyākṛta).These are fourteen kinds of extreme view based on self-view:[135]

(a) the world is permanent,
(b) the world is impermanent,
(c) the world is both-permanent-and-impermanent,
(d) the world is neither-permanent-nor-impermanent;
(e) the world is finite,
(f) the world is infinite,
(g) the world is both-finite-and-infinite,
(h) the world is neither-finite-nor-infinite;
(i) life (or soul) is the body,
(j) life is different from the body;
(k) after death the Tathāgata (the Buddha) exists,
(l) after death the Tathāgata does not exist,
(m) after death the Tathāgata both exists and does not exist,
(n) after death the Tathāgata neither exists nor does not exist.

These are all considered meaningless argumentation (P. papañca, Skt. prapañca),[136] and not to be declared (avyākata, avyākṛta).[137] The fading away of all such extreme view is the emptiness of the middle way.

(5) The middle way of neither the happiness of sense-pleasures nor the suffering of self-mortification. This refers

to the practice of the middle way – the noble eightfold way (ariya aṭṭhaṅgika magga).[138] According to MN 139 and MA 169, the noble eightfold way, leading to the realisation of nirvana, consists in practice that approaches neither of these two extremes: the happiness of sense-pleasures and the suffering of self-mortification.[139]

Accordingly, the emptiness that is based on the middle way of conditioned genesis eliminates all extreme views, and the practical way is the "noble eightfold way". This is not just an idea; it is a practical philosophy of life, based on the reality of the body and mind, to develop, to see the middle way, leading to the extinction of self-view and the realisation of nirvana. In early Buddhism, nirvana is expressed only in terms of the cessation of suffering, complete emptiness of self view, or of desire, hatred, and delusion. The uncompounded or unconditioned, nirvana, is beyond all arguments about existence and non-existence (= self-view); it is pointed to by the middle way of conditioned genesis. Consequently, compounded nature (conditioned genesis) and uncompounded nature (nirvana) are not opposed to each other as contrasting entities. No wonder, then, that conditioned genesis and nirvana are said to be profound, difficult to see, and connected with emptiness.

To summarise, the middle way of conditioned genesis centres on fading way from extreme self-view and is directly connected with the meaning of nirvana. Therefore, in early Buddhism there is a deep relationship between emptiness and the right view of the middle way.

In my view, conditioned genesis connects with both the arising and the ceasing of the world (suffering), so it indicates the emptiness of both time and space by emphasising the realisation of "time" (impermanence) as not of self. The arising (implying existence) and the ceasing (implying non-existence) show *time* as arising and the ceasing and *space* as existing and not existing. From non-existence to existence is arising, and from existence to non-existence is ceasing; or from future coming to present is arising, and from present going to past is ceasing. This arising and ceasing is *the passage of time* (impermanence) implying *the existence and non-existence of space* (the world). Thus, conditioned genesis mainly focuses on "time" as conditioned (P. saṅkhata, Skt. saṃskṛta); arising and ceasing indicate the emptiness of both time and space – neither arising nor ceasing as well as neither existence nor non-existence.

Chapter Two: The Practice of "Emptiness" in Early Buddhism

2.1. Emptiness and Samatha-vipassanā (calm and insight)

2.1.A. Development in both Samatha and Vipassanā

"Emptiness" (P. suññatā, Skt. śūnyatā) and "empty" (P. suñña, Skt. śūnya) have the meaning "not-self", and it is through insight into not-self that the emptiness of nirvana is attained. Not-self is emptiness in the sense of seeing the objective world as empty of self, and nirvana is emptiness as the attainment of a mind empty of craving. The connection between these two – seeing the objective world and the attainment – is "development" or "practice" (P. Skt. bhāvanā). Bhāvanā is the way (P. magga, Skt. mārga) to liberation (P. vimutti, Skt. vimukti), and emptiness is essential to that way.

The early Buddhist texts indicate that the Buddha, recognising the different situations, needs and abilities of people, established various ways and practices, such as "the four settings-up of mindfulness",[140] "the four right efforts",[141] "the four factors of psychic power",[142] "the five faculties",[143] "the five powers",[144] and "the seven factors of enlightenment",[145] but in the early stages of Buddhism, the foundation of the way of liberation or bhāvanā is the "noble eightfold way" (ariya-aṭṭhaṅgika-magga):[146]

1. right view (sammā diṭṭhi),
2. right thought (sammā saṅkappa),
3. right speech (sammā vācā),
4. right action (sammā kammanta),
5. right livelihood (sammā ājīva),
6. right effort (sammā vāyāma),
7. right mindfulness (sammā sati),
8. right concentration (sammā samādhi).[147]

The content of this noble eightfold way is summarised as three forms of training (tisso sikkhā): the training of morality (sīla-sikkhā), the training of mind (citta-sikkhā), and the training of wisdom (paññā-sikkhā);[148] or three classes (tayo khandhā): the class of morality (sīlakkhandha), of concentration (samādhikkhandha), and of wisdom (paññākkhandha).[149] In DN 16 Mahā-Parinibbāna Sutta and DA 2 there is mention of four sublimes (anuttarā) or truths (dhammā): morality (sīla), concentration (samādhi), wisdom (paññā), and liberation (vimutti),[150] and SA 565 and AN 4. 194 say there are four purifications: moral purification (sīla-pārisuddhi), mind-purification (citta-pārisuddhi), view-purification (diṭṭhi-pārisuddhi), and purification of liberation (vimutti-pārisuddhi).[151] These four sublimes (and truths) or four purifications indicate that the way of practice entails the trainings of morality, of mind (or concentration), and of view (or wisdom), in order to attain liberation.

Nevertheless, according to SA 816-823 and AN 3. 85-89 on the teaching of the three trainings,[152] both the training of mind (P. citta-sikkhā, Skt. citta-śikṣā) and the training of wisdom (P. paññā-sikkhā, Skt. prajñā-śikṣā) are directly for the extinction of craving or suffering, whether partly or completely. The training of mind or of concentration is for the aim of "samādhi" (concentration), and the training of wisdom or view is for the aim of "paññā" (wisdom, Skt.

prajñā). Thus, whether partial or complete in the "way to liberation" – the noble eightfold way – samādhi and paññā are the main factors in the cessation of craving or suffering.

Another summary of the way of practice recognises two categories: "samatha and vipassanā" (calm and insight, Skt. śamatha-vipaśyanā).[153] In samatha, "calm", the mind dwells on, or is aware of, one particular focus for the development of mental concentration or one-pointedness of mind (cittekaggatā); it is the "training of mind", emphasising "right concentration" (P. sammā samādhi, Skt. samyak-samādhi). Vipassanā, "insight", is seeing (vi + passati), completely and perfectly, phenomena as they really are. Vipassanā leads to the realisation of nirvana; it is the "training of wisdom", emphasising "right view" (P. sammā diṭṭhi, Skt. Samyag-dṛṣṭi).[154] By practising samatha one attains the meditative state of samādhi; by practising vipassanā one attains insight or paññā.

Although samatha and vipassanā are two different functions and methods of practice, they are not unrelated to each other: they help each other in the attainment of liberation. According to SA 560 and AN 4 170, there are four ways to combine the practices of samatha and vipassanā:

1. One develops vipassanā preceded by samatha,
2. One develops samatha preceded by vipassanā,
3. One develops both samatha and vipassanā, and
4. One emphasises developing samatha, if the mind is utterly unsettled.[155]

Consequently, samatha/samādhi and vipassanā/paññā can be explained differently, and can be practised in different order, but each helps the cultivation of the other, and both should be developed for the knowledge of nirvana (P. nibbāna-ñāṇa, Skt. nirvāṇa-jñāna).

Accordingly, the way of liberation directly relevant to emptiness is, above all, samatha and vipassanā, i.e. the development of samādhi and paññā. Concentrative meditation or samatha/samādhi leads to fading away or elimination of desires; like "emptiness" or "empty", it has the character of denial and negation: one becomes empty of desires. Insight or vipassanā/paññā is related to the notion of not-self and nirvana, and is also to some extent related to concentrative meditation; so it too is directly connected with emptiness. Thus, there is a deep relationship between emptiness and the practice of samatha-vipassanā or samādhi-paññā.

2.1.B. Samādhi

"Samādhi" means "meditative state of concentration" but is also a term for meditation in general. In early Buddhist texts there are various other terms denoting meditation. For example, in the explanation of one[156] of the "ten powers" (dasabalāni) of the Tathāgata (the Buddha), four terms – jhāna, vimokha (or vimokkha), samādhi, samāpatti – are listed together:

> The Tathāgata knows, as they really are, the fault, the purification, and the emergence of *meditation, liberation, concentrative meditation, attainment* (tathāgato jhāna-vimokha-samādhi-samāpattīnaṃ saṃkilesaṃ vodānaṃ vuṭṭhānaṃ yathābhūtaṃ pajānāti).[157]

Clearly the four terms – jhāna, vimokha, samādhi, samāpatti – are synonyms meaning "meditation", though literally they can be explained differently.

1. Jhāna (Skt. dhyāna), meaning "[a concentrative state of] meditation" refers specifically to the first to fourth jhānas.[158]

2. Vimokha or vimokkha (Skt. vimokṣa), "emancipation" or "liberation", consists of the eight vimokhas (aṭṭha vimokkhā): (1) the first jhāna, (2) the second jhāna, (3) the fourth jhāna, (4) the realm of the infinity of space (ākāsānañcāyatana), (5) the realm of the infinity of consciousness (viññāṇañcāyatana), (6) the realm of nothingness (ākiñcaññāyatana), (7) the realm of neither-perception-nor-non-perception (nevasaññā-nāsaññāyatana), and (8) the cessation of perception-and-feeling (saññā-vedayita-nirodha).[159] From (4) to (7) are also called the four non-physical jhānas (cattāro arūpā).[160]

3. Samādhi, "concentration", is of three kinds: (1) suññatā-samādhi (emptiness-concentration), (2) animitta-samādhi (non-appearance-concentration), and (3) appaṇihita-samādhi (aimless concentration).[161]

4. Samāpatti (= Skt.), "attainment", refers to "the nine gradual abiding attainments" (nava anupubbavihāra-samāpattiyo):[162] the four jhānas (cattāri jhānāni), the four non-physical jhānas, and the cessation of perception-and-feeling.

These four kinds of meditation (jhāna, vimokha, samādhi, samāpatti) are different in name, and indicate different stages of the meditative state of concentration. Other terms, such as "samāhita" (settled [of mind]), "cittass' ekaggatā" (or "cittekaggatā" one-pointedness of mind), and "vihāra" (state, abode) also refer to the concentrative state of meditation, but none of them is a member of a set of meditations, like the above four kinds. However, the most basic concentrative meditation relevant to emptiness in early Buddhism is the four jhānas. Whether samādhi is a factor in the noble eightfold way (as sammā samādhi), or in the five faculties (as samādhi-indriya), or in the five powers (as samādhi-bala), or in the seven factors of wisdom (as samādhi-sambojjhaṅga), or in the three trainings (as citta-sikkhā)[163] – in all of these the reference is to the four jhānas.

Again, from the process of the meditative practice, the first jhāna consists in calming (passaddhi) through the ceasing of speech (vācā niruddhā); the second jhāna is calming through the ceasing of thought and investigation (vitakka-vicārā niruddhā); the third through the ceasing of zest or joy (pīti niruddhā); and the fourth through the ceasing of in-breathing and out-breathing (assāsapassāsā niruddhā).[164] The practice of these four meditations develops stability of the mind (concentration) and of the body (the breathing, ānāpāna),[165] and aloofness from the five strands of sense-desire (pañca kāmaguṇā),[166] the five obstacles (pañca nīvaraṇāni)[167] etc. Hence, jhāna is closely connected with the aim of liberation (emptiness) from suffering or affliction.

Finally, there are many texts[168] which indicate that in the process of training in morality, concentration (or mind), and wisdom (or view), leading to liberation, the meditator attains only the fourth jhāna before attaining the three knowledges (tisso vijjā, te-vijjā),[169] or the six supernormal knowledges (cha abhiññā, chaḷabhiññā),[170] whose culmination is the wisdom of the extinction of affliction or suffering – nirvana.

Therefore, in the way of liberation, only four jhānas are necessary as a foundation in concentration or samatha, preparatory to the training in vipassanā.

2.1.C. Paññā

Paññā (Skt. prajñā) "wisdom", which is "insight into things as they really are", is in SN and SA the chief and leader on the way to liberation. SN 12. 23 reports the Buddha as saying:

> Monks, I say that the destruction (or extinction) of the flows (= afflictions, "āsavā") is for the one who knows, who sees, not for the one who does not know, who does not see. (jānato ham bhikkhave passato āsavānaṃ khayaṃ vadāmi no ajānato no appassato).[171]

Again, SA 223 says:

> I do not say that one who does not know and does not see dharma will attain the ending of suffering (我不說一法不知不識而得究竟苦邊).[172]

"To know" (P. Skt. jānāti) and "to see" (P. passati, Skt. paśyati) refer to "knowledge and vision of things as they really are" (yathābhūta-ñāṇadassana). This is prerequisite to liberation. Therefore, the "wisdom-faculty" (paññā-indriya) or the "noble knowledge" (ariyañāṇa) is the chief of the five faculties (pañca-indriyāni);[173] and "right view" (sammā diṭṭhi) is the leader or fore-runner (pubbaṅgama) in the noble eightfold way.[174]

There are other terms similar in meaning to paññā "wisdom", such as aññā (knowledge), ñāṇa (knowledge); and, referring to practice, dhammavicaya (investigation of dharma, second of the seven factors of wisdom, satta-bojjhaṅgā), vīmaṃsā (investigation, fourth of the four factors of psychic power, cattāro iddhi-pādā), and vipassanā (insight). Each of these is either "sekha sammādiṭṭhi" (right view of one in training) or "asekha sammādiṭṭhi" (right view of one who has perfected the training).[175]

However, in the case of the wisdom of right view, there are two kinds: "knowledge of dharma-status" (dhamma-ṭhiti-ñāṇa) and "knowledge of nirvana" (nibbāna-ñāṇa). As mentioned in section 1.4, SN 12. 70 and SA 347 report the Buddha as saying:

> Susīma, first [one comes to have] knowledge of dharma-status (the nature of phenomena, dhamma-ṭṭhiti-ñāṇa), afterwards [one comes to have] the knowledge of nirvana (nibbāna-ñāṇa).[176]

Knowledge of dharma-status is knowledge of conditioned genesis.[177] According to SN 12. 70 and SA 347, a person who attains this knowledge of dharma-status is also called "one who is wisdom-liberated" (paññā-vimutta),[178] and achieves this without the first five "supernormal knowledges" (pañcā-bhiññā),[179] or the four jhānas, or the arūpa (non-physical) meditations.[180] Since "knowledge of dharma-status" (dhammaṭṭhiti-ñāṇa) is liberation through wisdom (paññā-vimutti), it follows that "knowledge of nirvana" (nibbāna-ñāṇa) is "twofold liberation" (ubhatobhāga-vimutti).[181]

As stated in section 1.3 and 1.4, "right view", rightly seeing things as they really are, is to know and see the arising and ceasing of suffering, to see the four noble truths or conditioned genesis. This is to remove the view of self (emptiness), leading to realisation of nirvana (emptiness). Knowing and seeing things as they really are (conditioned genesis) is also achieved by seeing and knowing "impermanence" (anicca) or the "middle way" (majjhimā-paṭipadā) in the nature of life. In other words, one sees that compounded nature is "impermanent", so it is "suffering" (the first noble truth), and thus is "empty of self"; or one sees that conditioned genesis (compounded nature) is the "middle way", so it is connected with "emptiness" – nirvana.

Thus, this "right view" of emptiness (devoid of desires, empty of self, the middle way, nirvana) is crucial for the attainment of "liberation by wisdom" (paññāvimutti) and "liberation both ways" (ubhatobhāga-vimutti) in the practice of vipassanā (insight).

2.2. Emptiness and Mind-liberation or Mind-concentration

"Meditation" or "concentrative meditation" (samādhi) is closely connected with "emptiness" in a set of four kinds of "mind-liberation" (cetovimutti) in the Pāli SN 41. 7 or of "mind-concentration" (心三昧 xin-sanmei)[182] in its Chinese counterpart SA 567.[183]

SN 41. 7 is a conversation between the venerable Godatta and the housemaster Citta, whereas SA 567 is a conversation between the venerable Nāgadatta (那伽達多 Naqiedaduo) and the housemaster Citra (質多羅 Zhiduoluo). Also at MN 43 there is a discussion of these four mind-liberations by Sāriputta teaching Mahā-koṭṭhita.[184] According to SN 41. 7, the four kinds of mind-liberation are:

1. immeasurable mind-liberation (appamāṇa-cetovimutti),
2. nothingness-mind-liberation (ākiñcañña-cetovimutti),
3. emptiness-mind-liberation (suññatā-cetovimutti), and
4. signless mind-liberation (animitta-cetovimutti).

The same four are given at SA 567, but with the term cetovimutti "mind-liberation" replaced by 心三昧 xin-sanmei "mind-concentration".

It appears, however, that "mind-concentration" has the same meaning as "mind-liberation", because SN 41. 7 uses the term "animitta-*cetosamādhi*" (signless mind-concentration) to explain "animitta-*cetovimutti*" (signless mind-liberation):

> Sir, herein, a monk, by not attending (amanasikārā) to all signs, enters and abides in the "*signless mind-concentration*" (animittaṃ cetosamādhim). This, sir, is called the "*signless mind-liberation*" (animittā ceto-vimutti).[185]

The same content is seen at SN 40. 9, but with "mind-concentration" (cetosamādhi) instead of "mind-liberation" (cetovimutti).[186] Furthermore, "mind-concentration" (ceto-samādhi) is elsewhere also called "concentration" (samādhi or 三昧 sanmei).[187] According to SA 567, the housemaster Citra asks the venerable Nāgadatta, concerning the four kinds of mind-concentration:

> Are all these *concentrations* (三昧 sanmei) taught by the World-Honoured One (the Buddha) or are they the Venerable Sir's own teaching?
>
> The venerable Nāgadatta replies: These are taught by the World-Honoured One.

Thus, ceto-vimutti (mind-liberation), cetosamādhi or 心三昧 xin sanmei (mind-concentration), and samādhi or 三昧 sanmei (concentration) all have the same meaning: "the state of concentrative meditation" or "meditation".

According to both SA 567 and SN 41. 7, these four mind-liberations/mind-concentrations, which are closely connected with emptiness, can be either different in name and meaning, or the same in meaning but different in name.

The Pāli SN 41. 7 explains the different names and different meanings as follows.

1. "Immeasurable mind-liberation" (appamāṇa-cetovimutti) is meditation in which one dwells pervading (pharitvā viharati) the whole world with a mind full of the four immeasurables (catasso appamaññāyo): loving-kindness (mettā), compassion (karuṇā), empathic joy (muditā), and equanimity (upekkhā), free from hatred and suffering.

2. "Nothingness-mind-liberation" (ākiñcañña-cetovimutti) is meditation with the idea "there is nothing" (natthi kiñcīti); it is the "nothingness-attainment" (ākiñcañña-samāpatti) or the "realm of nothingness" (ākiñcaññāyatana), the third of the "four non-physical jhānas" (cattāro arūpā).

3. "Emptiness-mind-liberation" (suññatā-cetovimutti) is meditation that consists in reflecting (patisañcikkhati) on emptiness of self or of anything belonging to self. The text says:

> Venerable Sir, here a monk goes to the forest, or to the root of a tree, or to an empty place, and thus *reflects*: *This is empty of self or of anything belonging to self.* This, Venerable Sir, is called "*emptiness-mind-liberation*". (Idha bhante bhikkhu araññagato vā rukkhamūlagato vā suññāgāragato vā iti *patisañcikkhati. Suññam idam attena vā attaniyena vā ti.* Ayaṃ vuccati bhante *suññatā cetovimutti*).[188]

This also has the same meaning as the expression "empty world" discussed in section 1.2, but here it is connected with the "empty places" for practising the meditation of emptiness, such as a forest, the root of a tree, or an empty place. The Chinese counterpart says:

> What is emptiness-mind-concentration (空心三昧 kong xin-sanmei)? A noble disciple, observing things as they really are, sees that the world is empty. The world is empty. It is eternally, unchangingly devoid of self or of anything belonging to self. This is called emptiness-mind-concentration.[189]

Here a clear connection is made between "not-self" and "empty world", and it is said that this is unchangingly how it really is.

4. "Signless mind-liberation" (animitta-cetovimutti) consists in not reflecting (amanasikārā) on all signs, abiding in tranquillity of mind.

The "same meaning with different names" is explained as referring to "immovable mind-liberation" (akuppa-cetovimutti) in the Pāli, or "non-battle" (無諍 wuzheng)[190] in the Chinese version. The term "non-battle" may be a shortened form of "non-battle-mind-concentration" (araṇa-cittasamādhi), or "non-battle-state (araṇa-vihāra), or "non-battle-concentration" (araṇa-samādhi). The Pāli defines "immovable mind-liberation" as follows:

> Truly, that immovable mind-liberation is empty of desire, empty of hatred, empty of delusion. (sā kho pana akuppā cetovimutti suññā rāgena, suññā dosena, suññā mohena.)[191]

The Chinese counterpart gives the same definition for the term "non-battle", but adds some further expressions:

> Non-battle is empty of desire, empty of hatred, and delusion; empty of eternal, unchanging nature; empty of self or of anything belonging to self. (無諍者，空於

貪，空於恚，痴，空常住不變易，空非我，非我所)[192]

Here the "empty of desire, hatred, and delusion" of the "immovable mind-liberation" or "non-battle" has the same meaning as "kong sanmei" (空 三 昧 emptiness-concentrative meditation) or "suññatā-vihāra" (emptiness-abode) (see section 1.2). The "empty of self or of anything belonging to self" of the Chinese version has the same meaning as "emptiness-mind-liberation" or "emptiness-mind-concentration" (3, above), and also has the same meaning as in the teaching of "empty world" (see section 1.2).

Nirvana, the "uncompounded nature" (asaṃkhata-dhamma), is connected with insight into not-self, and is only expressed by "empty of desire, hatred and delusion";[193] consequently, the terms "immovable mind-liberation" (akuppa-cetovimutti) or "non-battle" (無 諍 wuzheng), "emptiness-concentrative meditation" (空 三 昧 kong sanmei) or "emptiness-state" (suññatā-vihāra), and "emptiness-mind-liberation" (suññatā-cetovimutti) or "emptiness-mind-concentration" (suññatā-cetosamādhi or 空心三昧 kong xin sanmei), combine with both nirvana and meditation, and thus refer to "twofold liberation" (ubhatobhāga-vimutti), i.e. wisdom (paññā) and concentrative meditation (samādhi). This "twofold liberation" is the "knowledge of nirvana" (nibbāna-ñāṇa) as indicated in SN 12. 70 and SA 347.[194]

According to SN 41. 7 and SA 567, "desire (rāga), hatred (dosa), delusion (moha)" represent all afflictions (āsavas). These three afflictions are the "cause of limitation" (pamāṇa-karaṇa), "obstacle or hindrance" (kiñcana), and the "cause of signs" (nimitta-karaṇa). The "cause of limitation" is the opposite of (1) "immeasurable (appamāṇena) mind-liberation (or mind-concentration)";

"obstacle or hindrance" is the opposite of (2) "nothingness (ākiñcañña) mind-liberation"; and "cause of signs" is the opposite of (4) "signless (animitta) mind-liberation". For the monk who has eliminated these three afflictions (desire, hatred, delusion), cutting them off at the root so they will not grow again in the future, this "immovable mind-liberation" (akuppa-cetovimutti or "non-battle" 無諍) is supreme over the other mind-liberations or mind-concentrations: in this case the two texts do not mention (3) "emptiness-mind-liberation/emptiness-mind-concentration". This is because "emptiness of desire, hatred, delusion" has the same meaning as, or is another expression for, "emptiness-mind-liberation/emptiness-mind-concentration". Thus, the final aim of these four mind-liberations/mind-concentrations is integrated in "emptiness-mind-liberation/ emptiness-mind-concentration", which is called "immovable mind-liberation/non-battle". In other words, the shared meaning of these four mind-liberations/mind-concentrations is "emptiness of desire, hatred, delusion" – the supreme "immovable mind-liberation/non-battle"; it indicates four different ways of practising meditation, of which the main one is "emptiness-mind-liberation/emptiness-mind-concentration" for the ultimate aim of liberation – nirvana. This is the same meaning under four different names. Thus one sees that "emptiness" and "purity of freedom from affliction (āsava)" are not separated.

The four kinds of mind-liberation/mind-concentration may be summarised and explained as follows: (1) immeasurable mind-liberation is meditation on loving-kindness, compassion, empathic joy, and equanimity for the whole world, to make the mind free from hatred and suffering – an exercise in imaginative thinking; (2) nothingness-mind-liberation and (4) signless mind-liberation are meditations consist in not reflecting on anything or on any sign; and (3) emptiness-mind-liberation is meditation that consists in seeing (passati) nature as it really is. This, fourth, emptiness-meditation, is "right view" or insight (vipassanā) into nature as "empty of self", and leads to "emptiness of desire, hatred, and delusion" – nirvana. Thus, of these four kinds of meditation, the main one is emptiness-meditation, incorporated in the supreme meditation, "immovable mind-liberation" (akuppa-cetovimutti) or "non-battle" (無諍 wuzheng). Hence, the meditative way for the aim of liberation centres on "emptiness".

"Emptiness", meaning "not-self" and "empty of desire, hatred, delusion" in the four mind-liberations or the four mind-concentrations, is deeply connected with the practice of meditation (cetovimutti/cetosamādhi/心三昧 xin-sanmei/samādhi/三昧 sanmei) that leads to liberation (vimutti). However, in practice this is attained by the stages of knowing and practice, or knowing as part of the practice, i.e. "right view" (sammādiṭṭhi = insight), "disgust (with worldly desires)" (nibbidā), "absence of desire" (virāga), and cessation (nirodha) or liberation (vimutti),[195] with emphasis on samatha (calm) and vipassanā (insight), leading to samādhi (concentrative meditation) and paññā (wisdom). This way of practice (samatha-vipassanā) is called suññatā-vihāra/空三昧 kong-sanmei (discussed in section 1.2) or suññatā-cetovimutti/空心三昧 kong xin-sanmei, combining the two terms, suññatā/空 kong (as insight/wisdom) and vihāra/三昧 sanmei/cetovimutti/心三昧 xin-sanmei (as calm/concentrative meditation).

The four ways of mind-liberation/mind-concentration are based on different meditative methods (cetovimutti/xin-sanmei) with the same meaning in the final attainment (emptiness) in the practice of "calm" (samatha) and "insight" (vipassanā) for the aim of concentrative meditation (samādhi) and wisdom (paññā). They follow four different attainments of "conscious attention", such as "the mind dwelling pervading (pharitvā viharati) the whole world with the four immeasurables", "not attending (amanasikārā) to anything or to any sign", and "insight (vipassanā) into emptiness", to establish "meditation" (cetovimutti/xin-sanmei) with four different names. They are classified as a set of meditations (cetovimutti/xin-sanmei), but the essence of them is emptiness-insight (empty of self or of all afflictions, āsavas) for ultimate liberation – nirvana.

Not only do their contents differ in name; even the same name can have different meanings: deep and simple. It may be that the names were originally used with their common meanings, but were then influenced by the level of understanding of those transmitting the teaching. Thus, these four kinds of meditation were different in name (according to the meditative method), but could also be the same in meaning, in referring to the final goal, to the complete achievement of emptiness: empty of desire, hatred, and delusion (empty of self view). As a result, "immeasurable", "nothingness", "signless", immovable", and "non-battle" came to be seen as different names for "emptiness", the complete extinction of afflictions (āsavas).

2.3. Emptiness, Three Concentrations (samādhī), and Three Kinds of Contact (phassa)

The four kinds of mind-liberation (or mind-concentration), classified as a meditative group, have a common meaning, which is "emptiness-mind-liberation", the ultimate goal. However, emptiness-mind-liberation does differ in practice from the others. The Chinese sutra, SA 80,[196] gives an explanation of the relationship between "emptiness-concentration" (空三昧 kong sanmei) and two of the three other kinds of samadhi, "signless concentration" (無相三昧 wuxiang sanmei) and "nothingness-concentration" (無所有三昧 wusuoyou sanmei); it does not mention "immeasurable concentration" (無量三昧 wuliang sanmei). This text (SA 80) has no Pāli counterpart. According to it, one who achieves emptiness-concentration can achieve signless concentration and nothingness-concentration, and fading away of pride (māna); but one who does not achieve emptiness-concentration cannot achieve the others.[197] Hence, the purifying view (right view) of "emptiness-concentration" is the leader, and also is the basis for attaining signless concentration and nothingness-concentration, leading to the fading away of pride. This teaching is called "the purifying view (知見清淨 zhijian qingjing) of the noble dharma-mark (聖法印 sheng fayin, Skt. ārya-dharma-mudrā, P. ariya-dhamma-muddā)", indicating that it is regarded as characteristic of the Buddha's teaching.[198]

In SA 80, emptiness-concentration, signless concentration, and nothingness-concentration are recognised as a group of meditations (called "the purifying view of the noble dharma-mark"). But there exist other groups of three, such as the "three concentrations" (tayo samādhī), the three contacts (tayo phassā), etc.

The three concentrations or samādhis are named at DN 33:

> Again, there are three concentrations (tayo samādhī): emptiness-concentration (suññato samādhi), signless concentration (animitto samādhi), and aimless concentration (appaṇihito samādhi).[199]

Here "nothingness-concentration" is replaced by "aimless concentration", a common situation. But when the Pāli and Chinese versions are compared, they show little agreement. First, these three concentrations are inconsistently present or absent in the two traditions. For example, MA 211 says: "Emptiness, aimless, signless: these three dharmas are different both in meaning and in name";[200] however its Pāli counterpart, MN 43, lacks this statement.[201] Conversely, SN 43.4 names three kinds of concentration: emptiness, signless and aimless,[202] but its Chinese counterpart lacks this set of terms.[203] Second, the order of the three concentrations is not always in agreement. For example, in MA 211 and DA 9 the order is "emptiness, aimless, signless",[204] whereas in SN 43.4, DN 33, and AN 3.163 the order is "emptiness, signless, aimless".[205] The signless and aimless concentrations are inconsistent in their order. For the above two reasons, one may speculate that although these three kinds of concentration were a common teaching in early Buddhism, the establishing of the three as a group of "samādhis" was quite late and already influenced by early Buddhist schools (Sectarian Buddhism; see page 1, note 1).

The reason for removing nothingness-concentration and substituting aimless concentration in the set of three concentrations is not clear. One might suggest that nothingness-concentration had already become one of the four non-physical (arūpa) attainments (samāpatti), thus losing the meaning relevant to "emptiness", and so gradually was neglected. A second possibility is that "nothingness-concentration" and "aimless concentration" have the same meaning in terms of their ultimate goal, but that in order to indicate the meaning relevant to emptiness, the "nothingness-attainment", which is one of the "four arūpa attainments", was distinguished from "aimless concentration", the state of disgust (nibbidā) with worldly desires, leading to the cessation of nirvana. Thus, "aimless concentration" became distinct from "nothingness-concentration".

These three kinds of "samādhi" are also called three liberations (tayo vimokkhā): suññato vimokkho, animitto vimokkho, and appaṇihito vimokkho, or three doors to liberation (tīṇi vimokkhamukhāni);[206] but these terms are not found in the four Nikāyas and the four Āgamas, so belong already to the period of the early Buddhist schools.

There is no clear explanation of the content of the three concentrations, except that the Chinese EA 24.10 does have a collective explanation of them,[207] which however, does not appear in its Pāli counterpart AN 3.163.[208] This Chinese text says:

> What is called "emptiness-concentration" (空三昧 kong sanmei)? By "emptiness" is meant observing all dharmas (the nature of phenomena) as empty (觀一切諸法, 皆悉空虛). This is called emptiness-concentration. What is called "signless concentration" (無相三昧 wuxiang sanmei)? By "signless" is meant that no sign (nimitta) can be seen in all dharmas. This is called signless concentration. What is called aimless concentration (無願三昧 wuyuan sanmei)? By "aimless" is meant no desire for all dharmas. This called aimless concentration.
>
> Thus, a monk who does not attain these three concentrations continues in the cycle of birth and death, and cannot become enlightened.

Here, the term "emptiness" or "emptiness-concentration" is defined as "observing (gaining insight into) the nature of phenomena as empty". However, the same term in the four mind-liberations or mind-concentrations is defined as (1) "reflecting on emptiness of self or of anything belonging to self", which is also the meaning of "empty world", as noted in section 1.2; and (2) "empty of desire, hatred, and delusion", which is also the meaning of "emptiness-concentration" (kong sanmei) or "emptiness-state" (suññatā-vihāra), as also indicated in section 1.2. Thus, "the nature of phenomena as empty" can be rendered as "the world as empty", meaning empty of self, and empty of desire, hatred, delusion: nirvana.

The question arises why the "immeasurable mind-liberation" (appamāṇa-cetovimutti) or "immeasurable concentration" (無量三昧 wuliang sanmei), one of the four kinds of mind-liberation (or mind-concentration), is not included along with the "three concentrations". It may be that, because the immeasurable mind-liberation, based on the "four immeasurables" (catasso appamaññāyo), was considered a "Brahma-meditative state" (brahma-vihāra) and a "family-meditative state" (kullaka-vihāra),[209] it was seen as not essential to liberation and therefore was neglected. This left only the three main ways of liberation out of the four mind-liberations, namely: emptiness (suññatā), signlessness (animitta), and nothingness (ākiñcañña).

As for the three kinds of contact (phassa), these are also related to the three concentrations. MN 44 says:

> Friend Visākha, when a monk has emerged from the "attainment of the cessation of perception and feeling" (saññāvedayitanirodhasamāpattiyā) three contacts contact him (tayo phassā phusanti): contact that is empty (suññato phasso), contact that is signless (animitto phasso), contact that is aimless (appaṇihito phasso).[210]

Its Chinese counterpart MA 211 reads as follows:

> A monk who has emerged from the "attainment of cessation" contacts three contacts. What are the three contacts? The first is immovable contact (不移動觸 buyidong chu); the second is nothingness-contact (無所有觸 wusuoyou chu); the third is signless-contact (無相觸 wuxiang chu).[211]

While these three contacts differ from the three concentrations, the names are clearly related, as the following table shows:

Three Concentrations		Three Contacts	
SA 80	DN 33, MA 211 etc.	MA 211	MN 44
emptiness	emptiness	immovability	emptiness
nothingness	aimless (or signless)	nothingness	signless
signless	signless (or aimless)	signless	aimless

Further information is provided in MN 105 and MN 106. Both of these texts say that after "immovability" (āṇañja) come the "realm of nothingness" (ākiñcaññāyatana) and the "realm of neither-perception-nor-non-perception" (nevasaññānāsaññāyatana).[212] In the Chinese MA 75, which is the counterpart of MN 106, the terms are "immovability" (不動 budong), the "realm of nothingness" (無所有處 wusuoyou chu), and the "realm of non-perception" (無想處 wuxiǎng-chù = 無相處 wuxiàng-chù, the realm of the mind that is signless).[213] The order of these three terms coincides with the order of the "three contacts" – "immovability", "nothingness", "signless" – so the two sets may be related. Here, the Pāli term for "immovability" is "āṇañja", i.e. different from the word "akuppa", also translated "immovability", in the term "immovable mind-liberation" (akuppa-cetovimutti).

Whether in the four mind-liberations/mind-concentrations or in the three concentrations/contacts, "emptiness" is deeply connected with the practice of meditation that leads to liberation (vimutti). Here again, "emptiness" has the two meanings of "not-self" and "empty of desire, hatred, delusion". In practice, however, as noted in section 2.2, this is attained by the way of knowing and practice (or knowing as part of the practice): right view (sammādiṭṭhi = insight), disgust (with worldly desires) (nibbidā), absence of desire (virāga), and cessation (nirodha) or liberation (vimutti).[214] The emphasis is on samatha (calm) and vipassanā (insight), leading to samādhi (concentrative meditation) and paññā (wisdom). This way of practice, "samatha-vipassanā", variously called emptiness-mind-liberation (suññatā-cetovimutti), emptiness-mind-concentration (kong xin-sanmei), emptiness-concentration (suññato samādhi/kong sanmei), etc., is the essential path to the ultimate liberation: nirvana.

2.4. Small and Great Emptiness

Emptiness is the principal topic of two Pāli texts, MN 121 and MN 122, titled "Discourse on Small Emptiness" (Cūḷasuññata-sutta) and "Discourse on Great Emptiness" (Mahāsuññata-sutta),[215] with corresponding Chinese versions, MA 190 小空經 Xiao-kong Jing and MA 191 大空經 Da-kong Jing respectively.[216] These two texts, edited under the heading "emptiness", are relevant to the texts SA 236 and MN 151 on the teaching of kong sanmei/suññatāvihāra, discussed in section 1.2, and appear to have been progressively edited by expanding on the practice of emptiness with concrete explanations. These two Emptiness-sutras, which have greatly influenced the development of Buddhist thought, differ in content regarding the practice of insight into emptiness.

2.4.A. "Discourse on Small Emptiness"

In the Pāli MN 121 and its Chinese counterpart MA 190, the Buddha begins the teaching by saying: "Ānanda, formerly and now I abide much in the state of emptiness (suññatāvihārena)". He concludes the discourse, according to MN 121, by saying that in the past, the future, and at present, those recluses (samaṇā) or brahmans (brāhmaṇā)

> who enter and abide in *the purified and incomparably highest emptiness* are precisely entering and abiding in the purified and incomparably highest emptiness. (*parisuddhaṃ paramānuttaraṃ suññataṃ* upasampajja viharissanti, sabbe te imaṃ yeva parisuddhaṃ paramānuttaraṃ suññataṃ upasampajja viharissanti.)[217]

The corresponding Chinese (MA 190) says that in the past, the future, and at present, all Tathāgatas (Buddhas)

> practise this true emptiness, which is without perversion, and is called "the ending of flow" (= affliction, āsava), "non-flow", "the uncompounded mind-liberation". (行此眞實空, 不顚倒, 謂漏盡, 無漏, 無爲心解脫.)[218]

In SA 236, this concentrative state of emptiness is said to be "the meditation of the elders" (上座禪住 shangzuo-chanzhu) (see section 1.2), but here, all Buddhas dwell much in this "emptiness-state". Thus, these texts (MN 121 and MA 190) provide a clue to why "emptiness" would go on to become a significant practice and attainment much emphasised in later Buddhism, e.g. in Mahāyāna.

Certain essential portions of the content of the "Discourse on Small Emptiness" are set out below. The layout follows the Pāli MN 121; the Chinese MA 190 is included for comparison (on the right side of the tables) where it is different and needs to be discussed. The numbers mark significant sections in the process of exposition. A blank section indicates no corresponding content. Sections

(3) to (6) are summarised so are not placed within the table; the remainder are given in full within the table. The numbers of the Pāli version indicate altogether ten sections; these have eight corresponding sections in the Chinese.

The Buddha, after saying that formerly as now he abides much in the state of emptiness, then says to Ānanda:

<table>
<tr><th>MN 121 (Pāli)</th><th>MA 190 (Chinese)</th></tr>
<tr><td colspan="2">(1) It is just like this Palace of Migāra's Mother (Migāramātu pāsādo), which is empty of elephants, cows, horses and mares (suñño hatthigavāssavaḷavena), empty of gold and silver (suñño jātarūparajatena), empty of assemblages of men and women (suñño itthipurisasannipātena); but there is only this that is not emptiness (atthi c' ev' idaṃ asuññataṃ), that is to say the oneness grounded on the assembly of monks (yadidaṃ bhikkhusaṃghaṃ paṭicca ekattaṃ).</td></tr>
<tr><td></td><td>Ānanda, that which is not there, I view that as empty, but what remains there, I view that as really existing. (阿難, 若此中無者, 以此故我見是空; 若此有餘者, 我見眞實有.)

Ānanda, this is called practising true emptiness, absence of perversion. (行眞實空, 不顚倒也.)</td></tr>
</table>

<table>
<tr><td colspan="2">(2) In the same way, Ānanda, a monk, not attending (amanasikaritvā) to the perception of village (gāmasaññaṃ), not attending to the perception of human beings (manussasaññaṃ), attends (manasikaroti) to oneness (ekattaṃ) grounded on the perception of forest (araññasaññaṃ).</td></tr>
<tr><td>His mind is satisfied with, calm in, settled on and released in the perception of forest.</td><td></td></tr>
<tr><td>He knows (pajānāti) thus: The distress (daratha) that might be based on the perception of village does not exist here; the distress that might be based on the perception of human beings does not exist here. But there is only this degree of distress (atthi c' evāyaṃ darathamattā), that is to say the oneness grounded on the perception of forest (yadidaṃ araññasaññaṃ paṭicca ekattan ti).</td><td>He knows thus (彼如是知): *The distress that may come from the perception of village, I do not have it; the distress that may come from the perception of human beings, I also do not have it. There is only this distress that comes from the oneness of the perception of forest. (若有疲勞, 因村想故, 我無是也; 若有疲勞, 因人想故, 我亦無是. 唯有疲勞, 因一無事想故.)</td></tr>
</table>

He knows: This perception is empty of the perception of village (suññaṃ idaṃ saññāgataṃ gāmasaññāya); this perception is empty of the perception of human beings (suññaṃ idaṃ saññāgataṃ manussasaññāya). But there is only this that is not emptiness (asuññataṃ), that is to say the oneness grounded on the perception of forest (yadidaṃ araññasaññaṃ paṭicca ekattan ti).	[He knows thus:] *This is empty of the perception of village, empty of the perception of human beings. But there is this that is not emptiness, that is only the perception of forest. (空於村想, 空於人想, 然有不空, 唯一無事想.)
He rightly perceives (samanupassati) that which is not there as empty of it (iti yaṃ hi kho tattha na hoti, tena taṃ suññaṃ samanupassati); but he knows (pajānāti) what remains there as "that being, this exists" (yaṃ pana tattha avasiṭṭhaṃ hoti, taṃ santaṃ idam atthīti pajānāti).	That which is not there, he views that as empty; but what remains there, he views that as really existing. (若彼中無者, 以此故, 彼見是空; 若彼有餘者, 彼見眞實有.)

Thus, Ānanda, this for him develops to be true, unperverted, purified realisation of emptiness (yathābhuccā avipallatthā parisuddhā suññatāvakkanti bhavati).	Ānanda, this is called practising true emptiness, absence of perversion. (行眞實空, 不顚倒也.)

*These two paragraphs are interchanged in the Chinese text (T 1, p. 737a).

According to sections (1) and (2) (above), "emptiness" does not mean "absolutely nothing". In effect, the text is saying: If in A there is not B, then I view A as empty of B; but if in A there remains C, then I view C as really existing in A. Thus, A is empty of B, but it is not empty of C. As MA 190 says:

> That which is not there, he views that as empty; but what remains there, he views that as really existing.

And MN 121:

> He rightly perceives that which is not there as empty of it; but he knows what remains there as "that being, this exists".

Consequently, the view of emptiness is that A includes both existence and non-existence, or negation and affirmation. This opposing of emptiness and non-emptiness to explain "emptiness" is a different way of presentation from that used in SA 236 and MN 151 on the teaching of kong-sanmei/suññatā-vihāra. In the text such understanding is called "practising true emptiness, absence of perversion" or "true, unperverted, purified realisation of emptiness" (suññatāvakkanti).

This practice of emptiness is meant for a monk living in the forest, so it starts from the perception of forest (araññasaññaṃ). The monk concentrates, attending to the perception of forest, not attending to the perception of village and human beings, and thus the "distress" (daratha) of the perception of village and human beings does not exist. However, since distress still exists in the perception of forest leading to the realisation of emptiness, the monk goes further with the practice of emptiness-insight, as follows:

(3) He, not attending to the perception of human beings and forest, attends to the perception of earth (paṭhavī-saññā). The distress that comes from the perception of human beings and forest does not exist, but distress that comes from the perception of earth remains. This is empty of the perception of human beings and forest, but not empty of the perception of earth. This practice is not mistaken, but is a true realisation of emptiness.

In the same way, practising in order, the monk goes further, concentratedly attending to:

(4) the *perception of the realm of infinite space* (ākāsānañcāyatana-saññā), not attending to the perception of forest and earth;

(5) attending to the *perception of the realm of infinite consciousness* (viññāṇañcāyatana-saññā), not attending to the perception of earth and the realm of infinite space;

(6) attending to the *perception of the realm of nothingness* (ākiñcaññāyatana-saññā), not attending to the perception of the realm of infinite space and the realm of infinite consciousness.

From here on, there are some disagreements between the Pali MN 121 and the Chinese MA 190 as shown below:[219]

MN 121	MA 190
(7) The monk, not attending to the perception of the realm of infinite consciousness and the realm of nothingness, attends to the *perception of the realm of neither-perception-nor-non-perception* (nevasaññānāsaññāyatana-saññaṃ) ...	
(8) And again, Ānanda, the monk, not attending to the perception of the realm of nothingness, not attending to the perception of the realm of neither-perception-nor-non-perception, attends to oneness grounded in the *signless mind-concentration* (animittaṃ cetosamādhiṃ)...	**(7)** And again, Ānanda, if a monk wishes to practise emptiness much, he, not attending to the perception of the realm of infinite consciousness and the realm of nothingness, attends only to the *mind-concentration of non-perception* (無想心定 wuxiǎng-xīn-dìng; comparison with the Pāli shows that this is in fact the term, *signless mind-concentration* "animita-cetosamādhi" 無相心定 wuxiàng-xīn-dìng).[220]

His mind is satisfied with, calm in, settled on and released in the signless mind-concentration.	
He knows thus: The distress that might be based on the perception of the realm of nothingness does not exist here; the distress that might be based on the perception of the realm of neither-perception-nor-non-perception does not exist here. But there is only this degree of distress, *that is to say the six sense-spheres which, conditioned by life, are grounded on this body itself* (imam eva kāyaṃ paṭicca saḷāyatanikaṃ jīvitapaccayā ti).	He knows thus: *The distress that may come from the perception of the realm of infinite consciousness, I do not have it; the distress that may come from the perception of the realm of nothingness, I also do not have it. There is only this distress, *that comes from the oneness of the "mind-concentration of non-perception"*. (唯有疲勞, 因一無想心定故.)
He knows: This perception is empty of the perception of the realm of nothingness; this perception is empty of the perception the realm of neither-perception-nor-non-perception. But there is only this that is not emptiness, *that is to say the six sense-spheres which, conditioned by life, are grounded on this body itself.*	[He knows thus:] *This is empty of the perception of the realm of infinite consciousness, empty of the perception of the realm of nothingness. But there is this that is not emptiness, *that is only the "mind-concentration of non-perception"*. (然有不空, 因一無想心定.)

He rightly perceives that which is not there as empty of it; but he knows what remains there as "that being, this exists"	That which is not there, he views that as empty, but what remains there, he views that as really existing.
Thus, Ānanda, this for him develops to be true, unperverted, purified realisation of emptiness.	Ānanda, this is called practising true emptiness, absence of perversion.
(9) And again, Ānanda, a monk, not attending to the perception of the realm of nothingness, not attending to the perception of the realm of neither-perception-nor-non-perception, attends to oneness grounded in the "*signless mind-concentration*" (animittaṃ cetosamādhiṃ).	
His mind is satisfied with, calm in, settled on and released in the signless mind-concentration.	

(10) He knows thus: This *signless mind-concentration* is compounded (abhisaṃkhato) and thought out (abhisañcetayito). But, he knows, whatever is compounded and thought out, that is impermanent, is of the nature of cessation (nirodhadhamman). When he knows thus, sees thus, his mind is liberated (cittaṃ vimuccati) from the *flow of sense-desire* (kāmāsavā), his mind is liberated from the *flow of becoming* (bhavāsavā), his mind is liberated from the *flow of ignorance* (avijjāsavā). In liberation arises the knowledge that his mind is liberated: He knows, birth is ended, noble conduct is established, done is what was to be done, there is no more of further becoming (Khīṇā jāti, vusitaṃ brahmacariyaṃ, kataṃ karaṇīyaṃ, nāparaṃ itthattāyāti pajānāti).	**(8)** He reflects thus: The *mind-concentration of non-perception* that I am based on is grounded on the compounded and the thought out. If this is grounded on the compounded and the thought out, I do not delight in this, nor seek this, nor abide in this. When he knows thus, sees thus, he is *mind-liberated* from the *flow of sense-desire*, *mind-liberated* from the *flow of becoming* and the *flow of ignorance*. Being liberated, he knows the liberation. He truly knows: birth is ended, noble conduct is established, done is what was to be done, there is no more of further becoming. (彼作是念:我本無想心定, 本所行, 本所思. 若本所行, 本所思者, 我不樂彼, 不求彼, 不應住彼. 如是知, 如是見, 欲漏心解脫, 有漏, 無明漏心解脫. 解脫已, 便知解脫. 生已盡, 梵行已立, 所作已辦, 不更受有, 知如眞.)

He knows thus: The distress that might come from the *flow of sense-desire* does not exist here; the distress that might come from the *flow of becoming* does not exist here; the distress that might come from the *flow of ignorance* does not exist here. But there is only this degree of distress, *that is to say the six sense-spheres which, conditioned by life, are grounded in this body itself.*	He knows thus: *The distress that may come from the *flow of sense-desire*, I do not have it; the distress that may come from the *flow of becoming* and of the *flow of ignorance*, I also do not have them. There is only this distress, *which exists in the six sense-spheres conditioned by the life of my body*. (唯有疲勞, 因我身六處命存故.)
He knows: This perception is empty of the *flow of sense-desire* (so: Suññam idaṃ saññāgataṃ kāmāsavenāti pajānāti); he knows: This perception is empty of the *flow of becoming* (suññam idaṃ saññāgataṃ bhavāsavenāti pajānāti); he knows: This perception is empty of the *flow of ignorance* (suññam idaṃ saññāgataṃ avijjāsavenāti pajānāti). But there is only this that is not emptiness, that is to say *the six sense-spheres which, conditioned by life, are grounded in this body itself.*	[He knows thus:] *This is empty of the *flow of sense-desire*, empty of the *flow of becoming* and of the *flow of ignorance*. But there is this that is not empty, *which exists only in the six sense-spheres in the life of my body*. (然有不空, 唯此我身六處命存.)

He rightly perceives that which is not there as empty of it. But he knows what remains there as "that being, this exists".	That which is not there, he views that as empty, but what remains there, he views that as really existing.
Thus, Ānanda, this for him develops to be true, unperverted, purified realisation of emptiness.	Ānanda, this is called practising true emptiness, without perversion. That is to say the ending of flow, non-flow, uncompounded mind-liberation.

*These two paragraphs in (7) and (8) are interchanged in the Chinese text (T 1, p. 737c).

Thus, the Pāli MN 121 has one more meditative stage than the Chinese MA 190: the perception of the "realm of neither-perception-nor-non-perception" (above, No. 7).

This may indicate that in the Chinese the "signless mind-concentration" (無 相 心 定 wuxiàng-xīn-dìng, animitta cetosamādhi) is the same state as the "realm of neither-perception-nor-non-perception", while in the Pāli MN 121 the "realm of neither-perception-nor-non-perception" is separated from the "signless mind-concentration". The reason for this is that in both MA 190 and MN 121 the "signless mind-concentration" is of two kinds: The first kind is "grounded on the compounded and the thought out" (see above No. 8 of MA 190, and No. 10 of MN 121), and the other kind is "mind liberated from the flow of sense-desire, becoming, and ignorance" (see above No. 8 of MA 190 and No. 10 of MN 121). The former means that the "signless mind-concentration" still has "distress" (daratha) so is not the final aim of "emptiness". In this case, if one does not see and know that "the compounded and thought out" of the "signless mind-concentration" is "impermanent" and "of the nature of cessation", one will delight in, seek, and abide in that state (see above No. 8 of MA 190 and No. 10 of MN 121). The other kind of "signless mind-concentration" is when one knows and sees that the compounded and thought out of the "signless mind-concentration" is "impermanent" and "of the nature of cessation"; and thus, not delighting in, seeking, and abiding in the state, one's mind is completely empty of the flow of sense-desire, becoming, and ignorance (see above No. 8 of MA 190 and No. 10 of M 121). This is to attain the liberation of wisdom (paññā) which is the supreme "immoveable mind-liberation" (akuppa-cetovimutti) as well as "emptiness mind-liberation" (suññatā-cetovimutti) in the "signless-mind-liberation" (animitta-cetovimutti), as indicated in the four kinds of "mind-liberation" (section 2.2).

As a result, *abiding* in the state of "signless mind-concentration" (the first kind) is the same as the "realm of neither-perception-nor-non-perception" given in the Pāli but not in the Chinese – though the Chinese version directly indicates two kinds of "signless mind-concentration". By contrast, the Pāli, after the "realm of nothingness", separately establishes the "realm of neither-perception-nor-non-perception", and then speaks of two kinds of "signless mind-concentration", leading to the extinction of the three kinds of flow.

Accordingly, there are two misplaced expressions in the Pāli, whether one is looking at the content or context of both the Pāli and the Chinese or comparing with the Chinese. They are as follows:

> (8). . . But there is only this degree of distress, <u>that is to say the six sense-spheres which, conditioned by life, are grounded on this body itself</u> (imam eva kāyaṃ paṭicca saḷāyatanikaṃ jīvitapaccayā ti).

> ... But there is only this that is not emptiness, that is to say the six sense-spheres which, conditioned by life, are grounded on this body itself.[221]

These are in No. 8 of the Pāli. The underlined words should be replaced by: "... that is to say the oneness grounded on the signless mind-concentration" (animittaṃ cetosamādhiṃ paṭicca ekattan ti). This will agree not only with the context of the first kind of "signless mind-concentration" but also with the whole context or content of practising "emptiness" in both the Pāli and Chinese texts.[222]

However, the words, "But there is only this degree of distress, that is to say the six sense-spheres which, conditioned by life, are grounded on this body", are also found in both No. 10 of the Pāli and No. 8 of the Chinese, as noted above. This indicates that one is empty of the three kinds of "flow" (āsavā) in the "signless mind-concentration", but the six sense-spheres (cha-āyatanāni) of the body in life are not empty before death. Nevertheless, in this case, one is freed from all afflictions of "flow", and knows: "Birth is ended, noble conduct is established, done is what was to be done, there is no more of further becoming".

Another section that needs to be deleted from the Pāli is No. 9. This section not only does not exist in the Chinese, as stated above; it also is repeated, and is out of keeping with the context of the whole text.

The two texts, do not use "attending to the *perception*" to refer to the practice of the "signless mind-concentration". Hence, each meditative state before the "signless mind-concentration" is a meditative state on "perception", whereas this final "signless mind-concentration" consists in not attending to any "perception".

To summarise, the realisation of emptiness in the "Discourse on Small Emptiness" proceeds step by step:

from "perception" to "non-perception", from "flow" to "non-flow", and from empty of various stages of perception to empty of the final non-perception – the "signless mind-concentration". In the beginning the way of practising this "signless mind-concentration" is different from that of 空三昧 kong-sanmei/suññatā-vihāra (see section 1.2), but the final attainment is the same. Thus, emptiness is deeply related to emptiness of distress (daratha) or of afflictions (āsavā), and stepwise progression through successive states of "oneness" that is not empty, with successive emptying out of previous attachments, is the characteristic of this "Discourse on Small Emptiness".

2.4.B. "Discourse on Great Emptiness"

Another important text relating to emptiness is MN 122, Mahāsuññata-sutta (Discourse on Great Emptiness) with its Chinese counterpart, MA 191.[223] The content is as outlined below.

(1) The Buddha tells Ānanda that it is not the case that a monk who delights in, or is intent on delighting in, his own group and other groups can easily attain the happiness of renunciation (nekkhamma-sukha), the happiness of aloofness (viveka-sukha), the happiness of calm (upasama-sukha), and the happiness of enlightenment (sambodha-sukha). On the other hand, a monk who dwells alone, remote from any group, is right thinking and following the most proper way for attaining those kinds of happiness without difficulty. As a result, that monk will abide entering the "liberation of mind that is temporal and pleasing" (sāmāyikā kantā cetovimutti), and the "liberation of mind that is non-temporal and immoveable" (asāmāyikā akuppā cetovimutti).

This teaching encourages monks to stay in empty places to practise meditation.

There is no explanation of the "liberation of mind that is temporal and pleasing" (sāmāyikākantā cetovimutti), and the "liberation of mind that is non-temporal and immoveable" (āsamāyikā akuppā cetovimutti). However, "liberation of mind that is non-temporal and immoveable" may refer to "immoveable mind-liberation" (akuppa-cetovimutti) or "emptiness-mind-liberation" (suññatā-cetovimutti), as noted in section 2.2.

(2) The Buddha indicates that he himself has achieved the ending of grief, sorrow, suffering, lamentation and despair, because he says:

> I do not behold one material form (rūpa), wherein is pleasure, wherein is found delight (nāhaṃ ekaṃ rūpaṃ pi samanupassāmi, yattha rattassa yatthābhiratassa).[224]

Thus the changing and becoming (vipariṇāmaññathābhāvā) of all material forms will not give rise to suffering.

> And Ānanda, this *abode (state) has been fully realised by the Tathāgata* (vihāro Tathāgatena abhisambuddho), that is to say, *by non-attention to all signs, attaining and abiding in inward emptiness* (sabbanimittānaṃ amanasikārā ajjhattaṃ suññataṃ upasampajja viharituṃ).[225]

Corresponding to the words, "by non-attention to all signs, attaining and abiding in *inward* emptiness", the Chinese (MA 191) has, "beyond all perceptions of material forms, practising the *outward* emptiness". (度一切色想, 行於外空.)[226]

Whether inward or outward, this emptiness-abode is attained "by non-attention to all signs" or by going "beyond all perceptions of material forms". Since the Tathāgata has attained this state (abode) of emptiness, his mind is free of any afflictions (suffering) even when monks, lay people etc. come to meet him or he teaches dharma to people.

This section of teaching indicates that the emptiness-abode has been attained by, certified by, and recognised by the Buddha, as the freedom of the one who has attained the "emptiness-abode".

(3) This is the main part of the teaching of emptiness-abode. If a monk wishes to enter the emptiness-abode, he should steady, calm, make one-pointed, and concentrate his mind precisely (the Chinese has: "持内心住,止令一定. "). According to the Pāli, this refers to practice of the four jhānas (meditations).

Then, the monk, based on jhāna, attends (manasikaroti) to four kinds of emptiness: 1. inward emptiness (ajjhattaṃ suññataṃ), 2. outward emptiness (bahiddhā suññataṃ), 3. emptiness both inward and outward (ajjhatta-bahiddhā suññataṃ), and 4. immovability (āṇañjaṃ).

According to the Chinese, practising these four kinds of meditative "attending" is done in order, and one reviews the practice until one fully purifies, abides in, and knows the attending to the four kinds of emptiness. However, the Pāli only mentions the four kinds of attending; it does not mention practising these four in order, but speaks of attending to the mind fully satisfied with (pakkhandati), pleased with (pasīdati), set on (santiṭṭhati), and freed in (vimuccati) the four kinds of attending. There is no definition of these four in either tradition, so we are left with no idea what is meant by this attending to the four kinds of emptiness.

(4) The condition of a monk abiding in the emptiness-abode is described thus: 1. He is clearly conscious

(sampajāna) that his mind is without the evil, unskilled states of covetousness and grief (nābhijjhādomanassā pāpakā akusalā dhammā) while walking, standing, sitting, and lying down. 2. He is clearly mindful (sampajāna) that he will not engage in any kind of worldly talk but only in talk relevant to nirvana. 3. He is clearly conscious that he will not think thoughts about sense-pleasures (kāmavitakka), malevolence (byāpādavitakka), and harming (vihiṃsā-vitakka), but will think thoughts about renunciation (nekkhammavitakka), non-malevolence (abyāpādavitakka), and harmlessness (avihiṃsāvitakka). 4. He is clearly mindful as to whether his mind is fading away from the five strands of sense-pleasures (pañca kāmaguṇā).[227] 5. He is clearly conscious of the arising (samudaya) and disappearance (atthagama) of the five groups of attachment (pañca upādānakkhandhā),[228] and he knows that he has got rid of "self-pride" (asmimāna).

(5) The affliction (upaddava) for teachers, pupils, and those of noble conduct (brahmacariya). A monk who lives in an empty place to practise meditation will backslide through the arising of evil unskilled states by associating with worldly people who crowd in on him. This is the affliction of teachers, pupils and those of noble conduct. It indicates that meditation may degenerate, so the monk should be aware of this, and should develop the complete achievement of emptiness-abode as an important task.

Finally, (6) the Buddha, as a teacher, teaches dharma to disciples for their welfare and happiness, out of compassion, so disciples should conduct themselves towards the teacher with friendliness, not hostility, and follow his teaching.

The emptiness-abode in the "Discourse on Great Emptiness", as outlined above, is related to the 空三昧 kong-sanmei (concentrative meditation of emptiness) of the 上座禪住 shangzuo-chanzhu (meditative abode of the elders) in SA 236. As noted in section 1.2, SA 236 indicates that a monk who wishes to abide in the shangzuo-chanzhu should practise mindfulness and extinction of craving and impure attachment when going for almsfood, receiving almsfood, leaving after walking for almsfood, and in everyday life in walking, standing, sitting, and reclining. This is called "purity of almsfood". Corresponding to this text (SA 236) is the Pāli MN 151 "Piṇḍapātapārisuddhi-sutta", but this text has more teaching, such as the teaching on the "five strands of sense-pleasures" (pañca kāmaguṇā), the "five hindrances" (pañca nīvaraṇā), the "five groups of attachment" (pañc' upādānakkhandhā), etc., which one can easily identify.[229] By contrast, emptiness-abode in the "Discourse on Great Emptiness" centres on four kinds of attending, emphasising emptiness of afflictions in everyday life, but it has much more content than SA 236 (and MN 151).

The practices described in the two discourses on emptiness differ in orientation. In the "Discourse on *Small Emptiness*" the practice proceeds vertically, step by step, providing oneness that is not empty, through the fading away of other perceptions in the process of practising emptiness, to total emptiness of kāmāsava (flow of sense-desire), bhavāsava (flow of becoming), and avijjāsava (flow of ignorance). This is regarded as "small emptiness". On the other hand, the "Discourse on *Great Emptiness*" proceeds horizontally from inner to outer, by way of four kinds of emptiness in attending, up to the "emptiness-abode". This is called "great emptiness".

In these two texts "emptiness" refers to "empty place" and "empty of affliction", and thus has a thoroughly practical character. These two "emptiness" texts therefore represent an early stage in the process whereby "emptiness" (e.g. in the four kinds of mind-liberation = cetovimutti/ mind-concentration = 心三昧 xin-sanmei) would subsequently become more and more emphasised in the development of Buddhist philosophy.

Conclusion

This study has shown that "emptiness", although not the main theme of the original teaching of the Buddha, is undeniably a unique teaching of the Buddha. His teaching dealt with the issue of attaining release from the "continuous cycle of death and rebirth" (saṃsāra), which was a common concern in Indian religious thought in his time. In this social context, the Buddha claimed to have actually achieved the ideal of release from saṃsāra, based on his discovery of the middle way (majjhimā paṭipadā) of conditioned genesis (paṭicca-samuppāda) that leads to nirvana and expresses the notion of emptiness. Thus, the meaning of emptiness increasingly becomes a prominent and important theme in Buddhist teachings.

Despite the fact that the teaching of the Buddha is connected with the notion of emptiness, the term "empty" (suñña) or "emptiness" (suññatā) is not as significant in early Buddhist texts as the three terms, "impermanent" (anicca), "suffering" (dukkha), and "not-self" (anatta).

The attitude to emptiness, and the use it is put to, is different, between early Buddhism and early Mahāyāna. In general, early Mahāyāna directly emphasises "emptiness", so that nothing can be admitted as an existent substance; e.g. in the *Prajñāpāramitā-sūtras* all dharmas are said to be "empty", which seems to be a synonym of "nirvana" (neither existence nor non-existence), and in his *Mūla-madhyamaka-kārikā* Nāgārjuna philosophically expresses the middle way of conditioned genesis through the use of emptiness. By contrast, in early Buddhism emptiness is a practical doctrine, based on the observed reality of our body-and-mind. It manifests as follows.

Three meanings of "emptiness" have been identified in the early Buddhist texts. First is the common meaning. This refers to the "empty place" (suññāgāra) in which the monk practises meditation to develop concentration (jhāna) and wisdom (paññā), and this leads to a symbolic use of "emptiness" to describe the resulting meditative state.

Second is the main meaning, which is "not-self". The wisdom of not-self (i.e. the realisation that the world is empty of self) is the basic insight (right view "sammā diṭṭhi") that leads to the mind becoming empty of craving or desire-hatred-delusion. Here, the early Buddhist texts state that the object (the world) is empty of self; they do not state that the object itself is empty.

Third is the ultimate meaning or broad sense, referring to nirvana, or the meditative state/abode of emptiness (空三昧 kong-sanmei/suññatā-vihāra). Nirvana is of uncompounded nature (asaṃkhata), that is completely empty of craving or desire-hatred-delusion; it is the ending of suffering. This realm is characterised neither as existence (arising) nor as non-existence (ceasing).

The early Buddhist texts prescribe two main ways to know emptiness (not-self and nirvana). The first is to see (insight) the nature of phenomena as "impermanent" (anicca), and the second is to see the nature of phenomena as the "middle way" (empty of the two extreme views). These two ways, leading to knowledge of the emptiness of not-self and to attainment of nirvana, are identified as "right view" in the development of wisdom (paññā).

The notion of "impermanence" and the "middle way" is based on the principal teaching of "conditioned genesis". Conditioned genesis indicates (1) the *compounded nature* (saṃkhata) that is impermanent and is the middle way, and (2) the *uncompounded nature* (asaṃkhata), i.e. nirvana. Thus, conditioned genesis is connected with emptiness (suññatāpaṭisaṃyutta).

The "right view" of insight (vipassanā) is essential for perfectly seeing (passati) and knowing (jānāti) the wisdom of "emptiness". This is also referred to as "knowledge and vision of things as they really are" (yathābhūta-ñāṇa-dassana). Although disciples of the Buddha do practise concentrative meditation (jhāna or samādhi) in "empty places", this meditation is limited to the mundane realms of rūpa (physical) and arūpa (non-physical). In early Buddhism it is not the principal requirement for liberation from saṃsāra, but is only an "expedient" or "skilful means" (upāya) in preparation for developing the wisdom of emptiness. Therefore, one who does not attain the jhānas (the four meditations) can still achieve "paññā-vimutti" (wisdom-liberation), and in early Buddhist thinking one must in practice first have the knowledge of conditioned genesis (i.e. dhammaṭṭhiti-ñāṇa "knowledge of the status of dharma"), and then come to have the knowledge of nirvana (nibbāna-ñāṇa). The Buddha's identification of "seeing" and "knowledge" (right view) as the basis for liberation is a unique teaching, not shared with other meditative traditions of his time.

Liberation by way of both "meditation" and "wisdom" is called "ubhatobhāga-vimutti" (twofold liberation). Related to this are various terms, such as "meditative state of emptiness/abode of emptiness" (kong-sanmei/suññatā-vihāra), "emptiness-mind-liberation/emptiness-mind-concentra-tion" (suññatā-cetovimutti/空 心 三 昧 kong-xin-sanmei), "immovable mind-liberation" (akuppa-cetovi-mutti), etc., each of which combines two terms: "emptiness" (as wisdom) and "meditation" (三 昧 sanmei, samādhi etc.). This twofold liberation is the final aim and essential path in the practice of "immeasurable mind-liberation" (appamāṇa-cetovimutti), "nothingness-mind-liberation" (ākiñcañña-cetovimutti), and "signless mind-liberation" (animitta-cetovimutti).

When one observes the use of "emptiness" in early Buddhist texts in the teachings of "empty world", "empty of desire-hatred-delusion", "empty of self or of anything belonging to self", "empty of two extreme views" (the middle way), "the four mind-liberations/mind-concentrations", "the three concentrations", "the Discourse on Small Emptiness" and "the Discourse on Great Emptiness", it becomes clear that "emptiness" or "empty" does not mean just denial, negation, devoidness, and voidness; it also means aloofness from affliction (āsava), suffering (dukkha), and distress (daratha) in the realm of purification and peacefulness. Thus, the term "emptiness" or "empty" is seen to be an essential notion in all phases of Buddhism: early Buddhism, the early Buddhist schools, and Mahāyāna.

It has been demonstrated in this study that the notion of "emptiness" arises from the early Buddhist sutras, though it is not initially a central theme of the teaching. The central teaching in early Buddhism is "conditioned genesis", this being the principle of the four noble truths, of not-self, etc. However, one can hardly escape the conclusion that "emptiness" is genuinely a teaching of the Buddha himself, and not simply a creation of the Mahāyāna.

Appendix: Three "emptiness-sūtras" in the Chinese Saṃyuktāgama and their reconstructed Sanskrit versions

For the three "emptiness-sūtras" in the Chinese Saṃyuktāgama, the Sanskrit originals have been reconstructed: SA 232 and SA 335 by LAMOTTE,[230] and SA 297 by TRIPĀṬHĪ.[231] These discourses were mentioned and partially translated from the Chinese on pages 14, 36-39. Here full translations from the Chinese are presented, together with the reconstructed Sanskrit, to facilitate further comparative study by interested scholars. The Sanskrit of SA 232 and SA 335, being retranslated from the Chinese, naturally matches closely with the English. The Sanskrit of SA 297, being reconstructed from fragmentary Sanskrit remains, disagrees slightly, but not as regards the teaching contained therein; constructed portions are shown in parentheses. Of these three emptiness discourses only SA 335 is lacking a Pāli counterpart.

(1) SA 232 Sanskrit text by LAMOTTE

1. Thus have I heard. At one time the Buddha (bhagavant) was staying at Jetavana, Ānāthapiṇḍika's park at Śrāvastī.	1. evaṃ mayā śrutam / ekasmin samaye bhagavāñ chrāvastyāṃ viharati sma jetavane 'nāthapiṇḍadasyārāme /

2. Then, a bhiksu named Samṛddhi came to where the Buddha was, saluted him by prostrating with his head to the ground and touching the feet of the Buddha, and sat down at one side. He then asked the Buddha:	2. atha samṛddhir nāma bhikṣur yena bhagavāṃs tenopajagāma / upetya bhagavatpādau śirasā vanditvaikānte nyaṣīdat / ekāntaniṣaṇṇo bhagavantam idam avocat/
3. It is said 'the world is empty', but in what regard, is it said that the world is empty?	3. śūnyo loka iti bhadanta ucyate / kiyatā śūnyo loka iti bhadanta ucyate/
4. The Buddha said to Samṛddhi:	4. evam ukto bhagavān samṛddhiṃ bhikṣum idam avocat /
5. Eye is empty, empty of eternal and unchanging nature, empty of anything belonging to self.	5. cakṣuḥ śūnyam / śāśvatenāvipariṇāma-dharmeṇa śūnyam / ātmīyena śūnyam /
6. Why is this so? This is nature as it is.	6. tat kasya hetoḥ / prakṛtir asyaiṣā /
7. Material forms, visual consciousness, visual contact, the feelings unpleasant or pleasant or neither-unpleasant-nor-pleasant that arise conditioned by visual contact are empty, empty of eternal and unchanging nature, empty of anything belonging to self.	7. rūpaṃ cakṣurvijñānaṃ yad apīdaṃ cakṣuḥsaṃ-sparśapratyayam udpadyate vedayitaṃ duḥkhaṃ vā sukhaṃ vāduḥkhāsukhaṃ vā / tad api śūnyam / śāsvatenāvipariṇāma-dharmeṇa śūnyam / ātmīyena śūnyam/

8. Why is this so? This is nature as it is.	8. tat kasya hetoḥ / prakṛtir asyaiṣā /
9. Ear, nose, tongue, body and mind are also thus.	9. evam eva śrotraṃ ghrāṇaṃ jihvā kāyo manaḥ /
10. This is called 'empty world'.	10. tasmāt śūnyo loka ity ucyate /
11. When the Buddha had taught this discourse, bhiksu Samṛddhi, having heard what the Buddha had said, was delighted, and put it into practice.	11. idam avocad bhagavān / samṛddhir bhikṣur bhagavato bhāṣitam abhinandyānumodya prakrāntaḥ //

(2) SA 297 Sanskrit text by TRIPĀṬHĪ

1. Thus have I heard. At one time, the Buddha was staying in the cow-herding community of the Kurus.	1. kuruṣu nidānam /
2. At that time, the Buddha said to the bhiksus:	2. tatra bhagavān bhiṣūn āmantrayati /
3. I will teach you the dharma, which is good in its beginning, middle, and end; which is of good meaning and good flavour, entirely pure, pure for the noble life,	3. dharmaṃ vo deśayiṣye ādau kalyāṇaṃ madhye kalyāṇaṃ paryavasāne kalyāṇaṃ yāvat prakāśyiṣye / yad uta mahāśūnyatānāma dharmaparyāyas tac chṛṇuta

	sādhu ca suṣṭhu ca manasi kuruta bhāṣiṣye /
4. namely: 'the discourse on the dharma of great emptiness'. Listen attentively, consider well, and I will teach you. What is the great discourse on the dharma of great emptiness? It is this: Because this exists, that exists; because this arises, that arises. That is to say: Conditioned by ignorance, activities arise; because of activities, consciousness arises, and so on ..., and thus arises this whole mass of suffering.	4. Mahāśūnyatādharma-paryāyāḥ katamāḥ / yad utāsmin satīdaṃ bhavaty asyotpādād idam utpadyate / yad utāvidyāpratyayāḥ saṃskārā yāvat samudayo bhavati /
5. Regarding [the statement] conditioned by birth, aging-and-death arise, someone may ask: Who is it that ages-and-dies? To whom do aging-and-death belong? And he may answer: It is the self that ages-and-dies. Aging-and-death belong to the self; aging-and-death are the self. To say that soul (jīva) is the same thing as body (śarīra), or to say that soul is one	5. jātipratyayaṃ jarāmaraṇam iti / tatra ko jarāmaraṇaṃ kasya vā jarāmaraṇam iti hi syuḥ praṣṭāra iti ya evaṃ vaded ayaṃ jarāmaraṇam asya vā jarāmaraṇam / yaś caivaṃ vadet taj jīvaṃ tac charīram anyaj jīvam anyac charīram / ubhayam

thing and body another, these have the same meaning, though they are expressed differently.	etad ekam / vyañjanam atra nānā /
For one who has the view which says that soul is the same thing as body, there is no point in the noble life. And for one who has the other view which says that soul is one thing and the body another, there is also no point in the noble life.	taj jīvaṃ tac charīram iti dṛṣṭau satyāṃ brahmacaryavāso na bhavati / anyaj jīvaṃ anyac charīram iti bhikṣavo dṛṣṭau satyāṃ brahmacaryavāso na bhavati /
The mind following neither of these two extremes, he moves rightly to the Middle Way, the noble, the supramundane, truly free of distortion, right view. This is to say: Conditioned by birth are aging-and-death.	ity etāv ubhāv antāv anupagamyāsti madhyamā pratipad āryā lokottarā yathābhūtā aviparītā samyagdṛṣṭiḥ / yad uta jātipratyayaṃ jarāmaraṇam /
6. And similarly conditioned are birth, becoming, attachment, craving, feeling, contact, the six sense-spheres, name-and-material form, consciousness, and activities.	6. evaṃ jātir bhava upādānaṃ tṛṣṇā vedanā sparśaḥ ṣaḍāyatanaṃ nāmarūpaṃ vijñānam /
7. Conditioned by ignorance, activities arise.	7. avidyāpratyayāḥ saṃskārā iti /

And if someone asks: Who is the activities? To whom do the activities belong? He may answer: The activities are the self; activities belong to the self.	tatra kaḥ saṃskārāḥ kasya vā saṃskārā iti hi syuḥ praṣṭāra iti ya evaṃ vaded ayaṃ saṃskārā asya vā saṃskārāḥ /
Thus for him, soul is the same thing as body, or he may says that soul is one thing and body another.	yaś caivaṃ vadet taj jīvaṃ tac charīram anyaj jīvam anyac charīram / ubhayam etad ekam / vyañjanam atra nānā /
For one who views soul and body as the same thing, there is no point in the noble life; and for one who says soul is one thing and body another, there is also no point in the noble life.	taj jīvaṃ tac charīram iti bhikṣa(vodṛ)ṣṭau (sa) tyāṃ brahmacaryavā(so na) bhavati / anyai jīvam anyac charīram iti dṛṣṭau satyāṃ brahmacaryavāso na bhavati /
Avoiding these two extremes, he moves rightly to the Middle Way, the noble, the supramundane, truly free of distortion, right view. This is to say: Conditioned by ignorance are activities.	ity etāv ubhāv antāv anupagamyāsti madhyamā pratipad āryā (lokottarā) yathābhūtā aviparītā samyagdṛṣṭiḥ / yad utāvidyāpratyayāḥ saṃskārāḥ /
8. Bhiksus! As to who ages-and-dies, and to whom aging-and-death belong, when ignorance fades away, and knowledge arises, aging	8. yataś ca bhikṣor avidyā viraktā bhavati vidyotpannā tasya ko jarāmaraṇaṃ kasya (vā jar)āmaraṇam/ avidyāvirāgād vidyotpādād

and death are cut off, and one knows they have been cut off at the root, like the cut off stump of a palm-tree, the nature of phenomenon in the future never to arise again.	evam asya taj jarāmaraṇaṃ prahīṇaṃ bhavati parijñātam ucchinnamūlaṃ tālamastakavad anābhavagatikam āyatyām anutpāda(dharma) /
9-10. Bhiksus! As to who is born, and to whom birth belongs, and so on ...; and as to who is the activities, and to whom the activities belong, when ignorance fades away, and knowledge arises, activities are cut off, and one knows they have been cut off at the root, like the cut off stump of a palm-tree, the nature of phenomenon in the future never to arise again.	9. yataś ca bhikṣor avidyā viraktā bhavati vidyotpannā tasya ko jātir bhava upādānaṃ tṛṣṇā vedanā sparśaḥ ṣaḍāyatanaṃ nāmarūpaṃ vijñānam / 10. tasya kaḥ saṃskārāḥ kasya vā (saṃ)skārāḥ / avidyāvirāgād vidyotpādād evam asya te saṃskārāḥ prahiṇā bhavanti parijñātā ucchinnamūlās tālamastakavad anābhava(ga)tikam āyatyām anutpādadharmāṇaḥ /
11. Bhiksus! When ignorance fades away and knowledge arises, in him ignorance ceases, and thus activities cease, and so on ..., and this whole mass of suffering ceases.	11. (ya)taś ca bhikṣor avidyā viraktā bhavati vidyotpannā tasyāvidyānirodhā(t) saṃskāranirodho yāvan mahato duḥkhaskandhasya nirodho bhavati /

12. This is called 'the discourse on the dharma of great emptiness'.	12. ayam ucyate mahāśūnyatānāma dharmaparyāyaḥ /
13. When the Buddha had taught this discourse, all the bhiksus, hearing what the Buddha had said, were delighted, and put it into practice.	13. dharmaṃ vo deśayiṣye ādau kalyāṇaṃ madhye pūrvavad iti me yad uktam idaṃ tat pratyuktam //

(3) SA 335 Sanskrit text by LAMOTTE

1. Thus have I heard. At one time, the Buddha was staying in a village of the cow-herding Kuru people.	1. evaṃ mayā śrutam / ekasmin samaye bhagavān kuruṣu viharati kalmāṣadamye nigame /
2. At that time, the Buddha said to the bhiksus:	2. tatra bhagavān bhikṣūn āmantrayati /
3. I will teach you dharma which is of good meaning and good flavour, entirely pure, pure for the noble life, namely: 'the discourse on emptiness in its ultimate meaning'. Listen attentively, consider well, and I will teach you.	3. dharmaṃ vo deśayiṣye ādau kalyāṇaṃ madhye kalyāṇaṃ paryavasāne kalyāṇaṃ svarthaṃ suvyañjanaṃ kevalaṃ paripūrṇaṃ pariśuddhaṃ paryavadātaṃ brahmacaryaṃ prakāśayiṣye / yad uta paramārthaśūnyatāsūtraṃ / tac chṛṇuta sādhu ca suṣṭhu ca manasikuruta bhāṣiṣye /

4. What is 'the discourse on emptiness in its ultimate meaning'? Bhiksus, when the eye arises, there is no place from which is comes; when is ceases, there is no place to which it goes.	4. paramārthaśūnyatāsūtraṃ katamam / cakṣur bhikṣava utpadyamānaṃ na kutaś cid āgacchati / nirudhyamānaṃ ca na kva cit saṃnicayaṃ gacchati /
5. Thus, the eye, being not real, arises; having arisen it ceases completely.	5. iti hi cakṣur abhūtvā bhavati bhūtvā ca pratigacchati /
6. It is a result of [previous] action but there is no doer; when these aggregates cease, other aggregates continue, except for this conventional dharma.	6. asti karmāsti vipākaḥ kārakas tu nopalabhyate ya imāṃś ca skandhān nikṣipaty anyāṃś ca skandhān pratisaṃdadhāty anyatra dharmasaṃketāt /
7. It is the same with the ear, nose, tongue, body, and mind.	7. evaṃ śrotraṃ ghrāṇaṃ jihvā kāyo mano vācyam /
8. They are exceptions to the conventional dharma. The meaning of conventional dharma is: Because this exists, that exists; because this arises, that arises, thus: Conditioned by ignorance are activities; conditioned by activities is consciousness, and so on ... and thus arises this whole mass of suffering.	8. anyatradharmasaṃketād iti / atrāyaṃ dharmasaṃketo yad utāsmin satīdaṃ bhavati / asyotpādād idam utpadyate / yad idam avidyāpratyayāḥ saṃskārāḥ / saṃskārapratyayaṃ vijñānam / yāvad evam asya kevalasya mahato duḥkhaskandhasyotpādo bhavati /

9. And again, when this does not exist, that does not exist; when this ceases, that ceases. When ignorance ceases, activities cease; when activities cease, consciousness ceases, and so on ... and thus ceases this whole mass of suffering.	9. tatrāsminn asatīdaṃ na bhavati / asya nirodhād idaṃ nirudhyate / yad utāvidyānirodhāt saṃskāranirodhaḥ / saṃskāranirodhād vijñānanirodhaḥ / yāvad evam asya kevalasya mahato duḥkhaskandhasya nirodho bhavati /
10. Bhiksus, this is called the discourse on the dharma of emptiness in its ultimate meaning.	10. ayaṃ bhikṣava ucyate paramārthaśūnyatā nāma dharmaparyāyaḥ /
11. When the Buddha had taught this discourse, the bhiksus, having heard what the Buddha had said, were delighted and put it into practice.	11. idam avocad bhagavān āttamanasas te bhikṣavo bhagavato bhāṣitam abhyanandan //

Notes

1 For a key to abbreviations, see p. 118.

2 There are different usages of the terms, "Original Buddhism", "Early Buddhism", and "Sectarian Buddhism" or "Early Buddhist schools". Here, following Yin Shun, "Original Buddhism" refers to the forty-five years of the actual teaching and activities of the Buddha, uncertainly dated to 511-431 BC (or 508-428 BC). "Early Buddhism" is applied to the period from the demise of the Buddha to about 300 BC, before the schism into Mahāsaṃghika and Sthavira. "Sectarian Buddhism" refers to the period from after the schism to before the emergence of early Mahāyāna Buddhism, about 300 BC to 100 BC. (Yin Shun, 原始佛教聖典之集成 [*The Formation of Early Buddhist Texts*], Zhengwen Chubanshe, Taipei, 1971, pp. 1-2, 867-879; and Yin Shun, 印度佛教思想史 [*A History of the Thought of Indian Buddhism*], Zhengwen Chubanshe, Taipei, 1993, pp. 8-9).

3 Yin Shun, 空之探究 [*A Study of Emptiness*] (Zhengwen Chubanshe, Taipei, 1986), pp. 143-148, 213.

4 Ibid., pp. 216-218, 243-253.

5 Hajime NAKAMURA, *Indian Buddhism: A Survey with Bibliographical Notes* (KUFS Publication, Japan, 1980), p. 248.

6 "Genshi Bukkyō ni okeru Kū", 空 Kū [*Emptiness*] (= 仏教思想 Bukkyōshisō [*The Thought of Buddhism*], vol. 2, ed. Bukkyōshisō Kenkyūkai) (Hirakuji Shoten, Kyoto, 1982), pp. 417-465.

7 *Kong zhi Tanjiu* (Zhengwen Chubanshe, Taipei, 1986), pp. 1-78.

8 NAKAMURA, p. 248.

9 Ibid., p. 247.

10 Also called Tāmraparṇīya or Taṃbapa[ṃ]ṇaka, the Buddhists of Tāmraparṇī (P. Tambapaṇṇi = Laṅka, Sīhaḷa; i.e. today's Sri Lanka Island). Cf. Étienne LAMOTTE, *History of Indian Buddhism: From the Origins to the Śaka Era* (trans. Sara

WEBB-BOIN) (1959; Institut Orientaliste de l'Université Catholique de Louvain, Louvain-la-Neuve, 1988), pp. 120, 301-302, 526, 536, 547, 786. Yin Shun points out that although the Tāmraśāṭīya tradition claims to represent the Theravāda (P.; Skt. Sthaviravāda) "the Teaching of the Elders", or Vibhajja-vāda (P.; Skt. Vibhajya-vāda) "the Teaching of the Distinction", it is actually a sub-sect of the Vibhajya-vādins, which derived from the Sthaviras (*Formation*, pp. 9-10; *History*, pp. 44-46).

11 Yin Shun, *Formation*, pp. 623, 681.

12 Yin Shun, *Formation*, pp. 89-102.

13 Councils of monks convened to determine the orthodox account of the Buddha's teaching.

14 Yin Shun, *Formation*, pp. 507, 622-625, 630-631, 695-696, 732, 788-791, 808, 861. For a review of this book and his 雜阿含經論會編 [*Combined Edition of Sūtra and Śāstra of the Saṃyuktāgama*], see MIZUNO Kōgen, "Zōagonkyō No Kenkyū To Shuppan" 雜阿含經の研究と出版 [*Studies and Publications of Saṃyuktāgama*], Bukkyō Kenkyū, 17 (1989), pp. 1-45.

15 Yin Shun, *formation*, pp. 622-625, 732, 788, 861.

16 Ibid., p. 732.

17 This and the following three paragraphs are based on ibid., pp. 629-702. Also Yin Shun points out that MA 191 and its counterpart MN 122 mention only "Sutta, Geyya, Veyyākaraṇa" (T 1, p. 739c; MN iii, p. 115); and that this is clear evidence that early Buddhism at one time recognized just three aṅgas (CSA i, "Preface", p. 2).

18 Ibid., pp. 629-702, 808, 861.

19 The view widespread among scholars that the Sutta-nipāta, Dhammapada, and Sagātha-vagga were composed earlier is based mainly on their relatively archaic language. But this reasoning is unsound, because verse always tends to be linguistically conservative in language.

20 Yin Shun (ed.), 雜阿含經論會編, 3 vols (1983; Zhengwen Chubanshe, Taipei, 1991). Vols. 1 and 2 are the collection of Sūtra; vol. 3 is the collection of Geya and Vyākaraṇa.

21 T 30, No. 1579, pp. 772c-868b. This text was translated from Skt. by Xuan Zang 玄奘 (596-664). The author is said to be

Maitreya or Maitreya-nātha, known as Maitreya Bodhisattva (c. 270-350 AD), but it is also regarded as Asaṅga (c. 310-390 AD) (Hajime NAKAMURA, *Indian Buddhism*, pp. 256, 264).

22 MIZUNO Kōgen (Tōho Shuppan, Osaka, 1986).

23 Compiled by Komazawa University, Tokyo (reprinted by 寶印佛經流通處, 修訂新版大藏經刊印處, Taiwan; date unknown).

24 Terms quoted from the texts are given in Chinese pinyin transcription and standard Pāli transcription. Where appropriate Sanskrit equivalents are also given.

25 SN v, p. 311. Its Chinese counterpart is SA 803: T 2, p. 206a (CSA ii, pp. 412-413).

26 E.g., MN i, p. 56; DN ii, p. 291; AN v, p. 111; for Chinese versions, see SA: T 2, pp. 20b, 77c, 184b, 255a, 206a; MA: T 1, pp. 550a, 553, 602b, 603b, 614b, 652a, 684c, 725b, 729a, 734a; DA: T 1, pp. 12b-c, 101b-c, 102a; EA: T 1, pp. 570a, 606b, 631c, etc.

27 SN 4. 6: SN i, pp. 106-107; SA 1089: T 2, p. 285b; ASA 28: T 2, p. 382a-b (CSA iii, pp. 34, 42).

28 SN i, pp. 180-181; SA 1183: T 2, p. 320a; ASA 97: T 2, p. 408a (CSA iii, pp. 158, 165).

29 AN 9. 40: AN iv, pp. 436-437; AN 10. 99: AN v, p. 207; MN 122: MN iii, pp. 115-116.

30 T 1, p. 725b.

31 E.g., SN 35. 197: SN iv, pp. 173-175; SA 1172: T 2, p. 313b; EA 31. 6: T 2, p. 669c (CSA i, pp. 333, 335).

32 SN i, pp. 106-107.

33 SA 1089: T 2, p. 285b; ASA 28: T 2, p. 382a-b (CSA iii, pp. 34, 42).

34 "Suññatā-vihāra" etc. will be discussed in section 1.2.

35 PED, p. 642.

36 The corresponding Skt. term may be śūnyatā-samādhi. In the Buddhist context "samādhi" does not mean only "concentration" or "concentrative meditation" . It refers to the "state of concentrative meditation", or "meditative state of concentration". For example, the four stages of dhyāna (P. jhāna, meditative state, literally "meditation") are the content of

"right concentration" (sammā samādhi). SN 45. 8: SN v, p. 10 (no SA counterpart). Cf. SA 784-785: T 2, pp. 203-204 (CSA ii, pp. 389-393).

37 Meditative state.

38 T 2, p. 57b (CSA i, pp. 280-281).

39 The Skt. term may be sthavira-vihāra.

40 MN iii, pp. 293-297. Another translation of the text is at EA 45 6: T 2, p. 773b-c (CSA i, pp. 280-281).

41 The words (vippasannāni kho te, Sāriputta, indriyāni parisuddho chavivaṇṇo pariyodato) are lacking in the Chinese counterpart, SA 236.

42 Another counterpart of SA 236 and MN 151 is Chinese EA 45. 6: T 2, p. 773b-c. This discourse uses the same term "kong-sanmei" (Skt. śūnyatā-samādhi) as SA 236, but states kong-sanmei is "the supreme samādhi" (第一三昧) and "the royal samādhi" (王三昧). Hence, these two Chinese versions are using the same term to correspond to suññatā-vihāra of the Pāli MN 151.

43 The Pāli MN 151 has similar content, but with additional information (MN iii, pp. 295-297). Here I indicate only the teachings common to the two texts. That the content of the Chinese SA 236 is much more concise than that of the Pāli MN 151 indicates that SA 236 was the earlier of the two versions.

44 Or avijjā, "ignorance, illusion, delusion".

45 MN iii, p. 294.

46 According to the Four Noble Truths (cattāri ariyasaccāni): 1. suffering (dukkha), 2. the arising of suffering (dukkhasamudaya), 3. the cessation of suffering (dukkhanirodha), and 4. the way leading to the cessation of suffering (dukkhanirodhagāminī-paṭipadā). SN 56. 11, 13-14: SN v, pp. 421, 425-426. SN 56. 11-12 has as counterpart SA 379 (CSA ii, pp. 106-109); but SN 56. 13-14 have no SA counterparts.

47 SN 23. 2, 38. 1, 43. 1: SN iii, p. 190; iv, pp. 251, 359, and their counterparts SA 122, 490, 890: T 2, pp. 40a, 126b, 224b (CSA iii, pp. 486, 374, 550).

48 Sn. v. 1119, p. 217.

49 SN iv, p. 54.

50 T 2, p. 56b (CSA i, pp. 276-277). This Chinese discourse has been reconstructed into Sanskrit by Étienne LAMOTTE, *Le Traité de la*

Grande Vertu de Sagesse de Nāgārjuna (Mahā-prajñāpāramitā-śāstra) avec une étude sur la Vacuité, tome IV (Louvain, 1976), pp. 2112-2113. This Skt. text also appears in the same author's, "Trois Sūtra du Saṃyukta sur la vacuité" *BSOAS*, 36 (1973), pp. 313-323. See also "Appendix" in this book.

51 Cha ajjhattikāni āyatanāni or cha indriyāni: eye, ear, nose, tongue, body, and mind-faculty.

52 Cha bāhirāni āyatanāni: visual, auditory, olfactory, gustatory, tactile, and mind-objects.

53 Cha viññāṇāni: visual consciousness, auditory, olfactory, gustatory, tactile, and mind-consciousness (consciousness of ideas).

54 Cha phassā: visual, auditory, olfactory, gustatory, tactile, and mental contacts.

55 Cha vedanā: visual, auditory, olfactory, gustatory, tactile, and mental feelings.

56 SN 35. 66, 68: SN iv, pp. 39-40 and SA 230: T 2, p. 56a-b, which is the counterpart of SN 35. 68, 66, and 65 (CSA i, pp. 275-276). Cf. SN 35. 82, 84: SN iv, pp. 52-53 and their counterpart SA 231: T 2, p. 56b (CSA i, p. 276).

57 SN 35. 106: SN iv, pp. 86-87, and its counterpart SA 218: T 2, p. 54c (CSA i, pp. 267-268).

58 There is in SN and SA a teaching about a connection between these "pleasant, unpleasant, neutral feelings" and "desire, anger, ignorance" (rāga, paṭigha, avijjā) respectively. SN 36. 6: SN iv, pp. 207-210 and its counterpart SA 470: T 2, pp. 119c-120b. See also SN 36. 3-4: SN iv, pp. 205-207 and their counterparts SA 468-469: T 2, pp. 119b-c (CSA ii, pp. 191-195).

59 SN ii, p. 104.

60 T 2, pp. 80b-81a (CSA ii, pp. 11-12).

61 SN 12. 21: SN ii, p. 28; SN 12. 61: SN ii, p. 95.

62 Referring to the first noble truth – suffering.

63 Referring to the second noble truth – the cause of suffering: craving (taṇhā). This is of three kinds: craving for sensuality (kāma-taṇhā), craving for becoming (bhava-taṇhā), and craving for non-becoming (vibhava-taṇhā).

64 The third noble truth – the cessation of suffering: nirvana.

65 The fourth noble truth – the noble eightfold way.

66 According to SN 12. 19 and its counterpart SA 294, nāma-rūpa is an external object (P. bahiddhā, Skt. bahirdhā "externally"). SN ii, pp. 23-25; T 2, pp. 83c-84a (CSA ii, pp. 31-32); cf. Skt. fragmentary version, Chandrabhāl TRIPĀṬHĪ, "Sūtra 12" *Fünfundzwanzig Sūtras des Nidānasaṃyukta* (Berlin, 1962), pp. 140-144.

67 Without the factors of (1) ignorance, (2) activities, (3) consciousness, (4) name-and-material form, (5) six sense-spheres, (6) contact, and (7) feeling. SA 283: T 2, p. 79a-b; Pāli counterpart, SN 12. 57: SN ii, p. 89; cf. SN 12. 55-56: SN ii, pp. 87-89. SA 285: T 2, pp. 79c-80b; Pāli counterpart, SN 12. 53 and 54: SN ii, pp. 86-87; cf. SN 12. 10: SN ii, p. 10. SA 366: T 2, p. 101a-b, but its Pāli counterpart, SN 12. 4: SN ii, pp. 5-9, has twelve factors. CSA ii, pp. 5, 8-9, 11, 82, 84.

68 Without the factors of (1) ignorance, (2) activities, (3) consciousness, (4) name-and-material form. SA 372: T 2, p. 102a-b; Pāli counterpart, SN 12. 12: SN ii, pp. 12-14. SA 352-354: T 2, p. 99a-c; but there are eleven factors in the Pāli counterparts, SN 12. 13-14, 71-81: SN ii, pp. 14-16, 129-130. CSA ii, pp. 72-75, 89-92.

69 Without the factors of (1) ignorance, (2) activities, (3) consciousness. SA 284: T 2, p. 79b-c; Pāli counterpart, SN 12. 58, 59: SN ii, pp. 90-91. CSA ii, pp. 6, 8.

70 Without the factors of (1) ignorance, (2) activities. SA 288: T 2, p. 81a-c; Pāli counterpart, SN 12. 67: SN ii, pp. 112-115. CSA ii, pp. 14, 16.

71 Without the factor of (1) ignorance. SA 367: T 2, p. 101b; Pāli counterpart, SN 12. 84: SN ii, p. 131; cf. SN 12. 82: SN ii, pp. 130-131. SA 356: T 2, p. 99c; but its Pāli counterpart, SN 12. 33: SN ii, pp. 56-59, has either eleven or twelve factors. SA 357: T 2, pp. 99c-100a; but twelve factors in Pāli counterpart, SN 12. 34: SN ii, pp. 59-60. SA 363: T 2, p. 100c; but twelve factors in Pāli counterpart, SN 12. 16: SN ii, p. 18. SA 367: T 2, p. 101b; Pāli counterpart, SN 12. 84: SN ii, p. 131; cf. SN 12. 82: SN ii, pp. 130-131. CSA ii, pp. 75-77, 80-81.

72 SN ii, p. 25.

73 T 2, p. 84b (CSA ii, pp. 34-35).

74 T 2, p. 85b (no SN counterpart; CSA ii, p. 40).

75 SN ii, p. 267. The Chinese counterpart, SA 1258 (T 2, p. 345b; CSA iii, p. 718) adds the italicized words: ". . . profound, enlightened, **connected with emptiness**, *in accordance with the dharma of conditioned genesis* (隨順緣起法)." Similar words occur at SA 293 (T 2, p. 83c; CSA ii, p. 25; no Pāli counterpart): "I teach to monks this Dharma: the noble, the supramundane, **connected with emptiness**, *in accordance with the dharma of conditioned genesis*". The quoted statement from SN 20. 7 is repeated at SN 55. 53 (SN v, p. 407); however, the corresponding Chinese SA 1033 (T 2, p. 270a; CSA iii, pp. 742-743), lacks the words. Other occurrences are at AN i, p. 72 and AN iii, p. 107. The term "suññatapaṭisaṃyuttā" (connected with emptiness) appears as "suññatāpaṭisaññuttā" at AN i, p. 72 and "suññatāpaṭisaṃyuttā" at AN iii, p. 107.

76 SN i, p. 136 (no SA counterpart). Its Chinese counterpart is EA 19. 1: T 2, p. 593a. See also MN 26 Ariyapariyesana-sutta: MN i, p. 167.

77 緣起隨順法. See also at SA 296: T 2, p. 84b (Pāli counterpart, SN 12. 20: SN ii, p. 25), and SA 1258: T 2, p. 345b (Pāli counterpart, SN 20. 7: SN ii, p. 267) (CSA ii, p. 35; iii, p. 718).

78 Cf. SA 262: "The emptiness of all activities, non-grasping, the extinction of craving, absence of desire: **nirvana** (一切諸行空寂, 不可得, 愛盡, 離欲, 涅槃)." (T 2, p. 66b-c; CSA i, pp. 54-56). Its Pāli counterpart, SN 22. 90, has: "the tranquillisation of all activities, the renunciation of all defilements, the extinction of craving, absence of desire, cessation: **nirvana** (sabbasaṅkhārasamathe sabbūpadhipaṭinissagge taṇhakkhaye virāge nirodhe nibbāne)." (SN iii, p. 133).

79 T 2, p. 83c; no Pāli counterpart (CSA ii, pp. 25-26).

80 SN ii, pp. 178-179; SN iii, pp. 149, 151.

81 The arising and ceasing of the world (lokassa samudayañca atthaṅgamañca) is the same as the arising and ceasing of suffering (dukkhassa samudayañca atthaṅgamañca) (SN 12. 43 Dukkha and 44 Loka: SN ii, pp. 71-73).

82 SN 23. 2: SN iii, p. 190; SA 122: T 2, p. 40a (CSA iii, p. 486).

83 SN 38. 1: SN iv, p. 251 and SN 43 1: SN iv, p. 359; SA 490: T

2, p. 126b and SA 890: T 2, p. 224b (CSA iii, pp. 374, 550).

84 The main root of suffering (dukkha) is craving (taṇhā) for sense-pleasures (kāma-taṇhā), for existence or becoming (bhava-taṇhā), and for non-existence or self-annihilation (vibhava-taṇhā). Thus, this "craving" is the same as desire (rāga), hatred (dosa), and delusion (moha).

85 SN ii, p. 124; T 2, p. 97b.

86 That is, "dhammaṭṭhitatā" (the status of dharma) (SN 12. 20: SN ii, p. 25 and its Chinese counterpart SA 296: T 2, p. 84b; also SA 299: T 2, p. 85b; CSA ii, pp. 35, 40). This term was mentioned in section 1.3, p. 19.

87 "Twofold" because comprising both liberation through wisdom (paññā-vimutti) and concentrative meditation (samādhi, state of concentrative meditation). SN 8. 7: SN i, p. 191; SA 1212: T 2, p. 330a; ASA 228: T 2, p. 457c; MA 121: T 1, p. 610b; EA 32. 5: T 2, pp. 676b-677b (CSA iii, pp. 201, 205 n. 7). See also Chapter two, p. 50.

88 SN 56. 29: SN v, p. 436; SA 382: T 2, p. 104b (CSA ii, p. 111).

89 "To be known accurately" (adjective, gerundive of parijānāti), cf. PED, p. 425.

90 That is, "craving" (taṇhā).

91 That is, nibbāna (Skt. nirvāṇa).

92 That is, the noble eightfold way. See Chapter two, pp. 43-44.

93 SA 785: T 2, p. 203a, counterpart of MA 189: T 1, p. 735 and MN 117: MN iii, p. 72 (CSA ii, pp. 390, 393 note 2).

94 SN 45. 1, 55: SN v, pp. 1-2, 31, and their counterparts, SA 749, 748: T 2, p. 198b (CSA ii, p. 369).

95 SN ii, p. 26. These words are lacking in the Chinese counterpart, SA 296: T 2, p. 84b (CSA ii, p. 35); however, that conditioned genesis implies compounded things are "impermanent, and subject to growth-and-decay (udaya-vyaya), fading away (virāga), cessation (nirodha), renunciation (paṭinissagga)" can be seen at SA 283, 284, 285: T 2, pp. 97a-80a (CSA ii, pp. 5-9) and many other texts in both Pāli and Chinese versions.

96 Pleasant feeling, unpleasant feeling, and neither-unpleasant-nor-pleasant feeling (neutral feeling). Each of them has six fields: visual, auditory, olfactory, gustatory, tactile, and mental feelings

through "contact" (phassa).

97 SN iv, pp. 216-217.

98 T 2, p. 121a-b (CSA ii, p. 199).

99 Pañca-khandha: 1. rūpa khandha (material form-aggregate), 2. vedanā khandha (feeling-aggregate), 3. saññā khandha (perception-aggregate), 4. saṃkhāra khandha (activity-aggregate), and 5. viññāṇa khandha (consciousness-aggregate). These emphasise psychological analysis. SN 12. Khandha Saṃyutta 1-158: SN iii, pp. 1-188 and their counterparts, SA 陰相應 (Yin Xiangying) 1-32, 256-272, 59-87, 33-58, 103-110: T 2, pp. 1a-7a, 64b-71c, 15b-22a, 7b-14b, 29c-35a (CSA i, pp. 1-212).

100 Saḷāyatana: the six sense-faculties (eye, ear, nose, tongue, body, and mind-faculty). These emphasise physiological analysis. SN 35. Saḷāyatana Saṃyutta 1-207: SN iv, pp. 1-204 and their counterparts SA 入處相應 (Ruchu Xiangying) 188-255, 1164-1177, 273-282, 304-342: T2, pp. 59b-63b, 310b-316c, 72b-78a, 86c-93b (CSA i, pp. 213-420).

101 Dhātu. The eighteen elements are: six sense-faculties with six external objects producing six consciousnesses. SN 14. Dhātu Saṃyutta 1-10: SN ii, pp. 140-149, and their counterparts, SA 界相應 (Jie Xiangying) 451-455: T 2, pp. 115-116, 125 (CSA ii, pp. 164-167).

102 SN 22. 43, 84, 7-8, 1-2: SN iii, pp. 42, 107ff, 16, 18-19, 1-9, and their counterparts SA 36, 271, 43-44, 107-108: T 2, pp. 8a-b, 71a-c, 10c-11a, 33a-34a (CSA i, pp. 141, 79f, 154-156, 193-197).

103 T 2, p. 71a (CSA i, p. 77).

104 SN iii, p. 157.

105 AN iv, p. 358. The same teaching is also found in the corresponding MA 56: T 1, p. 492a.

106 Or arrogance or self-conceit.

107 This term comes from vi + passati. "Passati" means "see", and the prefix "vi" here means "completely" "clearly" in an "intensifying sense" (PED, pp. 611, 627).

108 SN 22. 51: SN iii, p. 51 and its Chinese counterpart, SA 1: T 2, p. 1 (CSA i, p. 2); SN 35. 155-156: SN iv, p. 142 and the

Chinese counterpart, SA 188: T 2, p. 49b (CSA i, p. 215). According to CSA, the words 正觀 "right insight" in SA 1 should read 正見 "right view" (CSA i, p. 6). See also SA 58: T 2, p. 15a (CSA i, p. 177).

109 SN 22. 15: SN iii, p. 22; SA 9 and 10: T 2, p. 2a (CSA i, p. 13).

110 E.g. SA 316-318: T 2, p. 91a; SA 9-12: T 2, p. 2a-b (CSA i, pp. 404, 13-16), etc. SN 22. 15-20: SN iii, pp. 22-24; SN 22. 66-69: SN iii, pp. 76-78; SN 35. 1-12: SN iv, pp. 1-6; SN 35. 179: SN iv, p. 152, etc.

111 SN 22. 33, 69, 89: SN iii, pp. 34, 78, 127; SN 35. 85, 101, 193: SN iv, pp. 54, 82, 168. SA 9-12, 274: T 2, pp. 2a-b, 73a (CSA i, pp. 13-16, 335-336).

112 E.g. SN 22. 45: SN iii, p. 45.

113 SA 84: T 2, p. 21c (CSA i, p. 135; counterpart of SN 22. 45: SN iii, p. 45).

114 E.g. SN 22. 15-17, 45, 49, 59, 71-72, 76: SN iii, pp. 22-23, 45, 49f, 68, 80, 83. SN 35. 1-6, 71: SN iv, pp. 1-3, 43, etc. SA 199, 209, 248: T 2, pp. 51a, 52c-53a, 59c (CSA i, pp. 200, 254, 297), etc.

115 E.g. SA: T 2, pp. 1a-b, 20a, 35a, 50a-b, 92b, 153a, 315b, etc; MA: T 1, pp. 565c, 678a; EA: T 2, pp. 611c, 678c-679a, 689c, 702b, 715b-c, 728b, 745c, etc; see also T 1, Nos. 46, 73: pp. 836, 879; T 1, Nos. 5, 6, 7: pp. 172, 177, 206. These four terms are not found in DA.

116 T 2, p. 65b (CSA i, pp. 48-49). See also SA 110, 265, 291, 1175: T 2, pp. 35b, 68c, 82c, 315b; MA 153: T1, p. 672b, but its counterpart, MN 75, has: "as sickness, as swelling, as arrow, as pain, as illness" (MN i, p. 510), not mentioning the four terms.

117 SN iii, p. 167. See also MN 64: MN i, p. 435; AN 4. 124 and AN 9. 36: AN ii, p. 128, AN iv, pp. 422-423.

118 T 2, pp. 702b, 745c.

119 T 2, p. 715b-c: "無常者即是苦, 苦者即是無我, 無我者即是空也. 空者彼不(非)我有, 我非彼有."

120 T 2, pp. 678c-679a: "無常者即是苦, 苦者即是無我, 無我者即是空. 空者非有非不有, 亦復無我."

121 SN 22. 90 (SN iii, p. 135) and Nalanda Devanagari edition (vol. 2, p. 17; vol. 3, p. 353) read: na upādiyati nādhiṭṭhāti attā me ti

(does not cling to, does not insist on: it is my self).

122 SN ii, p. 17.

123 T 2, pp. 85c-86a (CSA ii, pp. 41-42).

124 T 2, pp. 59c-60a, and its counterpart, AN 4. 174 (173) and 175 (174): AN ii, pp. 161-164 (CSA i, p. 299). According to these, to say that in nirvana there is remainder, or there is no remainder, or there both is and is not remainder, or there neither is nor is not remainder is all meaningless argumentation (papañca).

125 SN iii, pp. 132-135 and its counterpart, T 2, pp. 66b-67a (CSA i, pp. 54-56).

126 Here the Chinese counterpart, SA 262, adds: "nirvana is cessation" (涅槃寂滅) (T 2, p. 66b).

127 Here the Chinese counterpart, SA 262, adds: "nirvana is cessation" (涅槃寂滅) (T 2, p. 66b).

128 T 2, pp. 84c-85a (CSA ii, pp. 36-37). Cf. the reconstructed fragmentary Sanskrit text "Sūtra 15" Chandrabhāl TRIPĀṬHĪ, *Fünfundzwanzig Sūtras des Nidānasaṃyukta* (Berlin, 1962) pp. 152-157. See also "Appendix" in this book.

129 SN ii, pp. 60-63.

130 T 2, p. 85c (CSA ii, p. 41) and its counterpart, SN 12. 46: SN ii, p. 75.

131 SN ii, p. 19 and its counterpart, SA 302: T 2, p. 86a-b (CSA ii, pp. 42-43).

132 T 2, p. 92c; cf. EA 37. 7: T 2, p. 713c (CSA i, p. 414).

133 This Chinese discourse has been reconstructed into Sanskrit by Étienne LAMOTTE, op. cit., pp. 2135-2137, also *BSOAS*, 36 (1973), pp. 313-323. See also "Appendix" of this book.

134 T 2, p. 72c (CSA i, p. 353).

135 SA 962-963: T 2, pp. 245b-246b, and their counterparts, MN 72: MN i, p. 483, and SN 33. 1-55: SN iii, 257-263, and ASA 196-197: T 2, pp. 444-445 (CSA iii, pp. 653-656).

136 SA 408: T 2, p. 109a, and its counterpart, SN 56. 8: SN v, p. 418 (CSA ii, p. 132).

137 SA 957-961: T 2, pp. 244a-245b, and their counterparts, SN 44. 9, 7, 8, 11, 10: SN iv, pp. 391-401, and ASA 190-195: T 2, pp. 443a-444c (CSA iii, pp. 649-653).

[138] See Chapter two, pp. 43-44.

[139] MN 139 Araṇavibhaṅga-sutta: MN iii, p. 231 and its Chinese counterpart, MA 169: T 1, 701b-c; SN 56. 11: SN v, p. 420f, but its Chinese counterpart, SA 379: T 2, p. 103c, lacks these words (CSA ii, pp. 106-108).

[140] Cattāro sati-paṭṭhānā: mindfulness of 1. the body, 2. the feelings, 3. the mind, and 4. phenomena. SN 47. Satipaṭṭhāna Saṃyutta 1-102: SN v, pp. 141-191, and their counterparts, SA 念處相應 (Nianchu Xiangying) 605-639: T 2, pp. 170c-177a (CSA ii, pp. 219-275).

[141] Cattāro sammappadhānā: 1. right effort in preventing evil states that have not arisen, 2. right effort in extinguishing evil states that have already arisen, 3. right effort in generating good states that have not arisen, 4. right effort in consolidating good states that have already arisen. SN 49. Sammappadhāna Saṃyutta 1-45: SN v, pp. 244-247. This section of text is lacking at SA (CSA ii, pp. 277-281); but the term 四正勤 (si zheng-qin) or 四正斷 (si zheng-duan) can be found in SA: T 2, pp. 14a, 19c, 87c, 176c, 182b, 183c, 184a, 185c, 186a, 188a, 192b, 213c, 221a; and the content is found at SA 647, 877-879: T 2, pp. 182b-c, 221a-b (CSA ii, pp. 294-295; iii, pp. 539-540).

[142] Cattāro iddhi-pādā: 1. will-concentration (chanda-samādhi), 2. effort-concentration (viriya-samādhi), 3. mind or thought-concentration (citta-samādhi), and 4. investigation-concentration (vīmaṃsā-samādhi). SN 51. 1 and 13: SN v, pp. 254, 268-269. This section of text (SN 51. Iddhipāda saṃyutta 1-86: SN v, pp. 254-293) is lacking at SA (CSA ii, pp. 283-289); but the term 四如意足 (si ru-yi-zu) can be found in SA: T 2, pp. 14a, 19c, 87c, 147b, 176c, 184b, 186c, 188b, 213c, 221c, 288c, 317b; and the content is found at SA 561: T 2, p. 147b (CSA iii, p. 453).

[143] Pañc' indriyāni: 1. faith-faculty (saddhindriya), 2. effort-faculty (viriyindriya), 3. mindfulness-faculty (satindriya), 4. concentration-faculty (samādhindriya), 5. wisdom-faculty (paññindriya). SN 48. Indriya Saṃyutta 8-10, 52: SN v, pp. 196-199, 228-229; SA 根相應 (Gen Xiangying) 646-647, 654-656: T 2, pp. 182b-c, 183b-c (CSA ii, pp. 294-295, 299)

[144] Pañca balāni: 1. faith-power (saddhābala), 2. effort-power

(viriyabala), 3. mindfulness-power (satibala), 4. concentration-power (samādhibala), 5. wisdom-power (paññābala). SN 50. Bala Saṃyutta 1, 56-57, 110: SN v, pp. 249, 251-253 (no SA counterparts). SA 力相應 (Li Xiangying) 673, 675: T 2, p. 185b-c and their counterparts, AN 5. 13, 15: AN iii, pp. 10-12 (CSA ii, pp. 310-311).

145 Satta bojjhaṅgā: 1. wisdom-factor of mindfulness (sati-sambojjhaṅga), 2. wisdom-factor of searching dharma (dhammavicaya-sambojjhaṅga), 3. wisdom-factor of effort (viriya-sambojjhaṅga), 4. wisdom-factor of zest (pīti-sambojjhaṅga), 5. wisdom-factor of tranquillity (passaddhi-sambojjhaṅga), 6. wisdom-factor of concentration (samādhi-sambojjhaṅga), and 7. wisdom-factor of equanimity (upekhā-sambojjhaṅga). SN 46. Bojjhaṅga Saṃyutta 1-175: SN v, pp. 63-139; SA 覺支相應 (Juezhi Xiangying) 704-747: T 2, pp. 189b-198a (CSA ii, pp. 329-365).

146 SN 56. 11-12: SN v, pp. 420-424, and their counterpart, SA 379: T 2, p. 103c (CSA ii, pp. 106-108).

147 According to SN 45. 8, "right view" is knowledge of the four noble truths; "right thought" is thought of detachment, of non-malice, and of harmlessness; "right speech" is avoiding lying speech, defamatory speech, abusive speech, and frivolous speech; "right action" is avoiding destroying life, stealing, and unchastity; "right livelihood" is living by right way of life; "right effort" is *the four right efforts*; "right mindfulness" is *the four settings-up of mindfulness*; and "eight concentration" is *the four jhānas* (SN v, pp. 8-10). These teachings are shared with SA version (e.g. SA 784 and 785: T 2, pp. 203a-204a; CSA ii, pp. 389-393).

148 SA 816-823: T 2, pp. 210a-211b (CSA ii, pp. 431-436), etc.; AN 3. 85-89: AN i, pp. 231-236, etc.

149 MN 44 Cūḷa Vedalla Sutta: MN i, p. 301, and its counterpart, MA 210: T 1, p. 788c classify the noble eightfold way into these three classes. In MN 44, "right speech, right action, and right livelihood" are classified as the "class of morality"; "right effort, right mindfulness, and right concentration" belong to the "class of concentration"; and "right view and right thought" are the

"class of wisdom". However, in MA 210, the class of wisdom is "right view, right thought, and right effort". Cf. also CSA ii, pp. 367-368 (quoting the commentary in the *Yogācāra-bhūmi-śāstra*).

[150] DN ii, p. 123; T 1, p. 17b.

[151] T 2, pp. 148c-149a (CSA iii, p. 458); AN ii, pp. 194-196.

[152] T 2, pp. 210c-211b (CSA ii, pp. 431-436); AN i, pp. 231-236.

[153] The different functions and methods of "samatha and vipassanā" are indicated in SA 560 (T 2, pp. 146c-147a; CSA iii, p. 452), and its counterpart, AN 4. 170 (AN ii, pp. 156-157).

[154] On "right view", which is to see (passati) the nature of phenomena as they really are, leading to nirvana, see section 1.4, above (pp. 24, 28, 32-33).

[155] T 2, pp. 146c-147a (CSA iii, p. 452), and its counterpart, AN ii, pp. 156-157.

[156] The third "power" in SA 684: T 2, p. 168c (CSA ii, p. 315); the seventh in AN 10 21: AN v, p. 34.

[157] SA 684: T 2, p. 168c and its Pāli counterpart, AN 10. 21: AN v, p. 34. The Pāli counterpart of SA 684 (T 2, p. 168b-169b) is in two parts: SN 22. 58: SN iii, pp. 65-66, and AN 10. 21: AN v, p. 32-36 (CSA ii, pp. 314, 318). See also the six powers of the Tathāgata at SA 686: T 2, p. 187b-c, and its Pāli counterpart AN 6. 64: AN iii, pp. 417-420 (CSA ii, pp. 318-319). Other texts: SN 52. 21: SN v, p. 305; MN 12: MN i, p. 70, etc.

[158] SN 16. 9: SN ii, pp. 210-211; Chinese counterpart, SA 1142: T 2, p. 302a (CSA iii, p. 578), etc.

[159] DN 33: DN iii, pp. 261-262; DA 9: T 1, p. 52b; others, DN 15, 16: DN ii, pp. 70-71, 111-112; MN 77: MN ii, pp. 12-13, etc.

[160] DN 33: DN iii, p. 224; DA 9: T 1, p. 50c.

[161] See section 2.3.

[162] SN 16. 10: SN ii, p. 216; SN 16. 12: SN ii, p. 222; AN 9. 33: AN iv, pp. 410-414; AN 9. 41: AN iv, p. 448. The term "nava anupubbavihāra-samāpattiyo" also appears as "nava anupubbavihārā" (nine gradual abodes) (AN 9. 32: AN iv, pp. 410; DN 33, 34: DN iii, pp. 265, 290). These two terms are lacking in the four Chinese Āgamas, but the content can be found at SA 474: T 2, p. 121a-b (CSA ii, p. 199); MA 85: T 1, p. 561a; DA 28: T 1, p. 110a-b; EA 24: T 2, p. 629a-b; and the

terms appear as 九次定 (jiu ci-ding) at T 1, No.13, p. 240a.

163 As "right concentration" (sammā samādhi): SN 45. 8 (SN v, p. 9); MN 141 (MN iii, p. 252). As "concentrative faculty" (samādhi-indriya): SN 48. 10 (SN v, p. 198); SA 655, 658 (T 2, pp. 183b, 184a; CSA ii, pp. 299, 300). As "concentrative power" (samādhi-bala): SA 675, 691 (T 2, pp. 185c, 188a; CSA ii, pp. 311, 321); AN 5. 14 (AN iii, p. 11). As "concentrative factor of wisdom" (samādhi-sambojjhaṅga): SA 715 (T 2, p. 193a; CSA ii, p. 341). As "training of mind" (citta-sikkhā): SA 817 (T 2, p. 210a; CSA ii, p. 432) and its counterpart, AN 3. 89 (AN i, pp. 235-236); SA 832 (T 2, p. 213c; CSA ii, p. 446) and its counterpart, AN 3. 88 (AN i, p. 235).

164 SN 36. 11: SN iv, p. 217.

165 This is relevant to the practice of "ānāpānasati" (mindfulness by in and out breathing) in seated meditation. See Chapter one, p. 8.

166 The desires of 1. visual sense, 2. auditory sense, 3. olfactory sense, 4. taste (gustatory) sense, and 5. touch (tactile) sense.

167 1. Sensuality (kāmacchanda), 2. ill-will (vyāpāda = byāpāda), 3. stolidity and drowsiness (thīna-middha), 4. over-balancing and worry (uddhacca-kukkucca), 5. doubt and uncertainty (vicikicchā).

168 MN 38, 39, 53, 76, 112, 125 (MN i, pp. 256 ff, 271 ff, 353 ff, 513 ff; MN iii, pp. 29 ff, 128 ff); MA 65, 80, 144 (T 1, pp. 506 ff, 551 ff, 652 ff).

169 1. Knowledge of one's past lives (pubbe-nivāsānussati-ñāṇaṃ vijjā), 2. knowledge of sentient beings' death and rebirth (= future lives) (sattānaṃ cutūpapāte ñāṇaṃ vijjā), 3. knowledge of the extinction of flows (= afflictions) (āsavānaṃ khaye ñāṇaṃ vijjā) (DN 33: DN iii, p. 220).

170 The psychic powers of 1. iddhi – appearing in various modes, such as producing many replicas of oneself; becoming invisible; passing without obstruction through solid walls; walking on water; flying through the air, 2. dibba-sota – divine hearing, 3. cetopariya-ñāṇa – reading other minds, 4. pubbe-nivāsa-anussati – knowing past lives, 5. dibba-cakkhu – divine sight, i.e. knowing future lives, 6. āsavakkhaya – extinction of flows (= afflictions) (DN 34: DN iii, p. 281).

171 SN ii, p. 29.

172 T 2, p. 55b (CSA i, p. 270).

173 SN 48. 52: SN v, pp. 228-229 and its counterparts, SA 654-656: T 2, p. 183b-c (CSA ii, pp. 298-299). See also SN 48. 51: SN v, pp. 227-228. Although the wisdom faculty is last in order of the five faculties, it leads the other four.

174 SN 45. 1, 55: SN v, pp. 1-2, 31 and their counterpart, SA 749, 748: T 2, p. 198b (CSA ii, p. 369); SA 787: T 2, p. 204a (CSA ii, p. 394) and its counterpart, AN 10. 104: AN v, pp. 212-214; AN. 10. 103: AN v, pp. 211-212 (cf. its counterpart, SA 786: T 2, p. 204a; CSA ii, p. 393).

175 SN 45. 13: SN v, p. 14 and its counterpart, SA 761: T 2, p. 200a (CSA ii, p. 376).

176 SN ii, p. 124; T 2, p. 97b (CSA ii, pp. 62-63).

177 SN 12. 20: SN ii, p. 25 and its Chinese counterpart SA 296: T 2, p. 84b, and in SA 299: T 2, p. 85b (CSA ii, pp. 35, 40).

178 Paññā-vimutta "the wisdom-liberated" in SN and SA also has similar content of both cittaṃ vimuttaṃ "the mind is liberated" and diṭṭhadhamma-nibbāna "experiencing nirvana in this very life" (or nirvana having known and understood the truth "dharma" by sight). Regarding paññā-vimutta, cittaṃ vimuttaṃ (Skt. cittaṃ vimuktam), and diṭṭhadhamma-nibbāna (Skt. dṛṣṭadharma-nirvāṇa), see SN 22. 58: SN iii, pp. 65-66 and SA 75: T 2, p. 19b; SN 22. 51: SN iii, p. 51 and SA 1: T 2, p. 1a; SN 115-116: SN iii, pp. 163-164 and SA 28: T 2, p. 6a (CSA i, pp. 123, 2-3, 36).

179 The sixth of the six supernormal knowledges (cha abhiññā, chaḷabhiññā) is achieved. See note 170.

180 In SA 347 it is without attaining the four dhyānas (jhānas) and the arūpa meditations (T 2, p. 97a; CSA ii, pp. 61-62); but in SN 12. 70 it is without the five supernormal knowledges and the states where the rūpa world (four jhānas) is transcended and the arūpa world is reached (SN ii, pp. 121-123).

181 Twofold because comprising (1) wisdom "paññā" or liberation through wisdom "paññā-vimutti" and (2) concentrative meditation (vimokkha "emancipation" or samāpatti "attainment", similar in meaning to jhāna and samādhi; see p. 46). Definitions of ubhatobhāga-vimutta and paññā-vimutta at

MN 70: MN i, pp. 477-478 and counterpart, MA 195: T 1, p. 751b. Regarding paññā-vimutta, neither version states that extinction of the āsavas is through jhāna or samādhi; both state: "but by his seeing with wisdom, his affliction-flows are destroyed (paññāya c' assa disvā āsavā parikkhīṇā honti)". Thus in early Buddhism, "wisdom" (right view) is the main factor for "liberation" from "affliction-flows".

182 The original Sanskrit term may be "cittasamādhi".

183 SA 567: T 2, pp. 149c-150a (CSA iii, pp. 462-463), and its counterpart, SN 41. 7: SN iv, pp. 295-297.

184 MN 43 (MN i, p. 297 f), but its counterpart MA 211 only names three samādhi "concentration": suññatā-samādhi (emptiness-concentration), animitta-samādhi (signless concentration), and appaṇihita-samādhi (aimless concentration) (T 1, p. 792a).

185 SN 41. 7: SN iv, p. 297.

186 SN 40. 9: SN iv, p. 268 f.

187 See section 2.3.

188 SN iv, p. 296-297. The same expression is found at MN 106: MN ii, p. 263.

189 T 2, p. 150a.

190 The original Sanskrit term may be "araṇa", which also means "peace" or "quietude" (PED, p. 76).

191 SN iv, p. 297.

192 T 2, p. 150a.

193 SN 43. 1: SN iv, p. 359; SA 890: T 2, p. 224b (CSA iii, p. 550).

194 SN ii, p. 124; T 2, p. 97b. See pp. 22-23.

195 SA 1: T 2, p. 1a, Pāli counterparts SN 22. 12 and 51: SN iii, pp. 21, 51; SA 8: T 2, p. 1c, Pāli counterpart SN 22. 9: SN iii, p. 19; SA 9: T 2, p. 2a, Pāli counterpart SN 22. 15: SN iii, p. 22; SA 28: T 2, p. 6a; SA 30: T 2, p. 6b, Pāli counterpart SN 22. 49: SN iii, pp. 48-50; SA 188: T 2, p. 49b, Pāli counterparts SN 35. 155-156: SN iv, p. 142; SA 726: T 2, p. 195b, Pāli counterpart SN 45. 2: SN v, p. 2; SA 727: T 2, p. 195c (CSA i, pp. 2, 6, 10-11, 13, 15, 36, 38-39, 41, 214-215, 195; CSA ii, pp. 352-354).

196 T 2, p. 20a-b (CSA i, pp. 127-128); two other translations are T 2, 103 (佛說聖法印經), p. 500a-b, and T 2, 104 (佛說法印經), p. 500b-c.

197 T 2, p. 20a-b.

198 According to FUJITA ("Emptiness", p. 442) and Yin Shun (*Emptiness*, p. 58), this text (SA 80) has been quoted in both Hīnayāna and Mahāyāna's Abhidharma books: T 26, pp. 25a, 73b; T 27, p. 541c; T 30, p. 792a; T 32, pp. 281c, 332c, 362b, 363b, 365a, etc.

199 DN iii, p. 219.

200 T 1, p. 792a.

201 MN i, pp. 292 ff.

202 SN iv, p. 360.

203 SA 890: T 2, p. 224a-b (CSA iii, p. 550).

204 T 1, p. 792a and p. 50b.

205 SN iv, p.360; DN iii, p. 219; AN i, p. 299.

206 Eg. Paṭisambhidāmagga (in Khuddaka-nikāya), ii, pp. 35, 48, 65-67. PED, p. 632.

207 T 2, p. 630b.

208 AN i, p. 299 f.

209 Cf. PED, pp. 494, 223.

210 MN i, p. 302.

211 T 1, p. 792a.

212 MN ii, pp. 254-255; MN ii, pp. 262-264.

213 T 1, pp. 542b-543a.

214 See note 195.

215 MN iii, pp. 104-109 and pp. 109-118. In their English translations Horner, and Ñāṇamoli and Bodhi see *cūḷa* and *mahā* as referring to *sutta* rather than to *suññatā*.

216 T 1, pp. 736c-738a and pp. 738a-740c.

217 MN iii, p. 109.

218 T 1, p. 737c.

219 MN iii, pp. 107-109; T 1, p. 737c.

220 Cf. also SA 272: T 2, p. 72a-b (CSA i, p. 84) and its counterpart, SN 22. 80: SN iii, p. 93.

221 MN iii, pp. 107-108.

222 Cf. FUJITA, "Emptiness", pp. 454-455.

223 MN iii, pp. 109-118; T 1, pp. 738a-740c.

[224] MN iii, p. 111.
[225] MN iii, p. 111.
[226] T 1, p. 738b.
[227] Visual, auditory, olfactory, gustatory, and tactile sense-pleasures.
[228] 1. Material form (rūpa), 2. feeling (vedanā), 3. perception (saññā), 4. activities (saṃkhārā), and 5. consciousness (viññāṇa).
[229] MN iii, pp. 295-297.
[230] T 2, pp. 56b-c, 92c (CSA i, pp. 276-277; 414). Étienne LAMOTTE, *Le Traité de la Grande Vertu de Sagesse de Nāgārjuna (Mahā-prajñāpāramitā-śāstra) avec une étude sur la Vacuité*, tome IV (Louvain, 1976), pp. 2112-2113, 2135-2137; see also the same author's "Trois Sūtra du Saṃyukta sur la vacuité" *BSOAS*, 36 (1973), pp. 313-323.
[231] T 2, pp. 84c-85a (CSA ii, pp. 36-37). Chandrabhāl TRIPĀṬHĪ, "Sūtra 15", Fünfundzwanzig Sūtras des Nidānasaṃyukta (Akademie-Verlag, Berlin, 1962), pp. 152-157.

Bibliography

(1) Piṭaka

I. Original Texts of Piṭaka

A. Pāli texts

Dīgha-nikāya, 3 vols. (PTS, 1889-1910).

Majjhima-nikāya, 4 vols. (PTS, 1888-1925).

Saṃyutta-nikāya, 6 vols. (PTS, 1884-1904).

Aṅguttara-nikāya, 6 vols. (PTS, 1885-1910).

Sutta-nipāta (PTS, 1913).

Nālandā Devanāgarī Pāli Series (3 vols in DN and in MN, 1958; 4 vols in SN, 1959, and in AN, 1960), ed. by J. Kashyap (Pāli Publication Board, Bihar Government, India).

PaliText, version 1.0 (CD-ROM, published by the Dhammakaya Foundation, Thailand, 1996). This is based entirely on the PTS edition.

Chaṭṭha Saṅgāyana, version 1.1 (CD-ROM, published by Vipassana Research Institute, India, 1997). This is based on the texts agreed on at the Sixth Council (Chaṭṭha Saṅgāyana) held in Myanmar during 1954-1956.

B. Chinese texts

"Dīrghāgama" (長阿含經), T 1, No. 1 (新文豐出版社 Xinwenfeng Publisher, Taiwan, reprinted 1983).

"Madhyamāgama" (中阿含經), T 1, No. 26 (Xinwenfeng Publisher, Taiwan, reprinted 1983).

"Saṃyuktāgama" (雜阿含經), T 2, No. 99 (Xinwenfeng Publisher, Taiwan, reprinted 1983).

"別譯雜阿含經" ["Additional Translation of Saṃyuktāgama"], T 2, No. 100 (Xinwenfeng Publisher, Taiwan, reprinted 1983).

"Ekottarāgama" (增一阿含經), T 2, No. 125 (Xinwenfeng Publisher, Taiwan, reprinted 1983).

"Yogācāra-bhūmi-śāstra" (瑜伽師地論), T 30, No. 1579 (author named as Maitreya or Maitreya-nātha, c. 270-350 AD, but ascribed to Asaṅga, c. 310-390 AD; translated from Skt. by 玄奘 Xuan Zang, 596-664 A.D.) (Xinwenfeng Publisher, Taiwan, reprinted 1983).

雜阿含經論會編 Za-ahan Jing-lun Huibian [*Combined Edition of Sūtra and Śāstra of the Saṃyuktāgama*] (ed. by 印順 Yin Shun) (1983; 正聞出版社 Zhengwen Chubanshe, Taiwan, 1991).

C. Reconstructed Sanskrit texts

TRIPĀṬHĪ, Chandrabhāl, *Fünfundzwanzig Sūtras des Nidānasaṃyukta* (Akademie-Verlag, Berlin, 1962).

LAMOTTE, Étienne, *Le Traité de la Grande Vertu de Sagesse de*

Nāgārjuna (Mahā-prajñāpāramitā-śāstra) avec une étude sur la Vacuité, tome IV (Louvain, 1976), pp. 2112-2113, 2135-2137.

----- "Trois Sūtra du Saṃyukta sur la vacuité" *BSOAS*, 36 (1973), pp. 313-323.

II. Translations from original texts of Piṭaka

A. English translations from Pāli

Dialogues of the Buddha (Dīgha-Nikāya), 3 vols. (tr. by T. W. and Mrs. C. A. F. Rhys Davids) (PTS, reprinted 1977).

Thus Have I Heard: The Long Discourses of the Buddha (Dīgha-Nikāya) (tr. by Maurice WALSHE) (Wisdom Publications, London, 1987).

Middle Length Sayings (Majjhima-Nikāya), 3 vols. (tr. by I. B. Horner) (PTS, reprinted 1975-77).

The Middle Length Discourses of the Buddha: A New Translation of the Majjhima-Nikāya (tr. by Bhikkhu Ñāṇamoli and Bhikkhu Bodhi) (Buddhist Publication Society, Kandy, Sri Lanka, 1995)

The Book of the Kindred Sayings (Saṃyutta-Nikāya), 5 vols. (tr. by Mrs. C. A. F. Rhys Davids and F. L. Woodward) (PTS, reprinted 1975-80).

The Book of the Gradual Sayings (Aṅguttara-Nikāya), 5 vols. (tr. by F. L. Woodward and E. M. Hare) (PTS, reprinted 1972-1982).

Minor Anthologies I (Dhammapada, and the Sutta-Nipāta) (tr. by F. Max Muller and V. Fausboll) (PTS, reprinted 1980).

B. Japanese translations

南伝大藏經 Nanden Daizōkyō [The Southern Tripiṭaka], 65 volumes, 70 fascicules (ed. by Junjirō Takakusu) (Daizō Shuppan Kabushiki Kaiha, Tokyo,1935-1941).

"Agonbu" (阿含部), 國譯一切經 Kokuyaku Issaikyō, vols. 1-5 (translated from the four Chinese Āgamas) (Taitō Shuppansha, Tokyo, 1970).

C. Chinese translations

漢譯南傳大藏經 Hanyi Nanchuan Dazangjing [*Chinese translations of Pāli texts*], vols. 1-47 ... (ed. by 元亨寺漢譯南傳大藏經編譯委員會, Taiwan) (published by 元亨寺妙林出版社, Taiwan, 1990 ...)

(2) General

CONZE, Edward, *Buddhist Thought in India: Three Phases of Buddhist Philosophy* (George Allen and Unwin, London, 1962).

COLLINS, Steven, "Self and non-Self in early Buddhism", (review of J. Perez-Remon, *Self and Non-Self in Early Buddhism*, 1981), *Numen: International Review for the History of Religions*, 29 (December 1982), pp. 250-271.

DARGYAY, Lobsang, "What is non-existent and what is permanent is śūnyatā", *Journal of Indian Philosophy*, 18 (March 1990), pp. 81-91.

ECKEL, Malcolm D., "Gratitude to an empty savior: a study of the concept of gratitude in Mahāyāna Buddhist philosophy", *History of Religions*, 25 (August 1985), pp. 57-75.

FUJITA, Kotatsu, "原始仏教における空" Genshi Bukkyō ni okeru Kū ["Emptiness in Early Buddhism"], 空 Kū [*Emptiness*] (= 仏教思想 Bukkyōshisō [*The Thought of Buddhism*] vol. 2, ed. by Bukkyōshisō Kenkyūki) (Hirakuji Shoten, Japan, 1982), pp. 417-465.

GOMEZ, Luis O., "Proto-Mādhyamika in the Pāli canon", *Philosophy East and West*, vol. XXVI, No.2 (April 1977), pp. 137-165.

HAYASHIMA, Kyōshō, 初期仏教と社会生活 Shoki Bukkyō to Shakai Seikatsu [*Early Buddhism and Social Life*] (Iwanami Shoten, Tokyo, 1964).

HOPKINS, Jeffrey, *Emptiness Yoga: the Middle Way Consequence School* (ed. Joe Bransford Wilson) (Snow Lion Publications, Ithaca, N.Y., 1987).

----- *Meditation on Emptiness* (assistant ed. Elizabeth Napper) (Wisdom Publications, London, 1983).

HUMPHREYS, Christmas, *Studies in the Middle Way* (Luzac, London, 1946).

----- *Studies in the Middle Way: Being Thoughts on Buddhism Applied* (G. Allen and Unwin, London, 1959).

KALUPAHANA, David J., "The Explanation of Paṭiccasamuppāda", *Buddhist Philosophy: A Historical*

Analysis (The University of Hawaii Press, Honolulu, 1976), pp. 26-35.

KOCHUMUTTAM, Thomas, "Śūnyatā and Tathatā: Emptiness and Suchness", *Journal of Dharma: An International Quarterly of World Religions*, 6 (January-March 1981), pp. 18-33.

LAMOTTE, Étienne, *History of Indian Buddhism: From the Origins to the Śaka Era* (trans. Sara WEBB-BOIN) (1959; Institut Orientaliste de l'Université Catholique de Louvain, Louvain-la-Neuve, 1988).

LAW, B. C., "Formulation of Pratītyasamutpāda", *Journal of the Royal Asiatic Society of Great Britain and Ireland* (1937), pp. 287 f.

MAEDA, Egaku, 原始仏敎聖典の成立史研究 Genshi Bukkyō Seiten no Seiritsushi Kenkyū *A History of the Formation of Original Buddhist Texts* (Sankibō Busshōrin, Tokyo, 1964).

MATSUO, Hosaku, *The Logic of Unity: the Discovery of Zero and Emptiness in Prajnaparamita Thought* (tr. by Kenneth K. Inada) (State University of New York Press, Albany, 1987).

MITCHELL, Donald W., "The No-Self Doctrine in Theravāda Buddhism", *International Philosophical Quarterly*, vol. IX, No. 2 (June 1969), pp. 248-260.

MIYAMOTO, Shoson, 中道思想及びその発達 Chūdō Shisō oyobi sono Hattatsu [*The Middle Way Doctrine and its Development*] (Hozokan, Tokyo and Kyoto, 1944).

----- 根本中と空 Kompon-chū to Kū [*The Fundamental Middle and Śūnyatā*] (Dai-ichi Shobō, Tokyo, 1943).

MIZUNO, Kōgen, *Primitive Buddhism* (translated, annotated and compiled by Kosho Yamamoto) (Karin Bunko, Ube, 1969).

----- "雜阿含經の研究と出版" Zōagonkyō No Kenkyū To Shuppan ["Studies and Publications of Saṃyuktāgama"], *Bukkyō Kenkyū*, 17 (1989), pp. 1-45.

----- *Buddhist Sutras: Origin, Development, Transmission* (1982; sixth printing, Kōsei Publishing Co., Tokyo, 1995)

NAKAMURA, Hajime, *Indian Buddhism: A Survey with Bibliographical Notes* (KUFS Publication, Japan, 1980).

NARAIN, H., "Śūnyavāda: A Reinterpretation", *Philosophy East and West*, vol. XIII (1964), pp. 311-338 .

STRENG, Frederick J., *Emptiness: A Study in Religious Meaning* (Abingdon Press, Nashville, New York, 1967).

THOMAS, Edward J., *The History of Buddhist Thought* (Alfred A. Knopf, New York, 1933).

UEDA, Shizuteru, "Emptiness and Fullness: Śūnyatā in Mahāyāna Buddhism", (tr. by J. W. Heisig and F. Greiner), *The Eastern Buddhist*, 15 (Spring 1982), pp. 9-37.

WARDER, A. K., "On the Relationships between Early Buddhism and other Contemporary Systems", *Bulletin of the School of Oriental and African Studies*, vol. XVIII, No. 1 (1956), pp. 43-62.

YADAV, Bibhuti S., "Negation, Nirvana and Nonsense", *Journal of the American Academy of Religion*, 45 (December

1977), pp. 451-471.

Yin Shun (印順), 原始佛教聖典之集成 Yuanshi Fojiao Shengdian zhi Jicheng [*The Formation of Early Buddhist Texts*] (Zhengwen Chubanshe, Taiwan, 1971).

----- 空之探究 Kong zhi Tanjiu [*A Study of Emptiness*] (Zhengwen Chubanshe, Taiwan, 1986).

----- 印度佛教思想史 Yindu Fojiao Sixiang Shi [*A History of the Thought of Indian Buddhism*] (Zhengwen Chubanshe, Taiwan, 1993).

(3) Reference

"Agonbu" (阿含部), 大藏經索引 Daizōkyō Sakuin, vol. 1 (Index to the Chinese Āgamas, compiled by Komazawa University, Tokyo) (reprinted by 寶印佛經流通處, 修訂新版大藏經刊印處, Taiwan; data unknown).

AKANUMA, Chizen, *The Comparative Catalogue of Chinese Āgamas & Pāli Nikāyas* (Hajinkaku-Shobō, Nagoya, Japan, 1929).

佛光大辭典 Fo Guang Dacidian [*Fo Guang Great Dictionary*], 8 vols. (Fo Guang Shan Buddhism, Taiwan, 1988)

MIZUNO, Kogen, 南伝大藏經総索引 Nanden Daizōkyō Sō Sakuin [General Index to Pāli Texts] (Tōhō Shuppan, Japan, 1986).

MOCHIZUKI, Shinkō, 望月佛教大辞典 Mochizuki Bukkyō Daijiten 10 vols. (Sekaiseiten kangōkyōkai, Kyoto, 1945-63).

NAKAMURA, Hajime, 佛教語大辞典 Bukkyōgo Daijiten

[*Great Dictionary of Buddhist Terms*] (Tokyo Shoseki, Japan, 1989).

RHYS DAVIDS, T. W., and STEDE, William (eds.), *Pali-English Dictionary* (Oriental Books Reprint Corporation, New Delhi, 1975; orignally published by PTS, 1921-25)

TAKASAKI, Jikidō (ed.), 仏教・インド思想辞典 Bukkyō Indo Shisō Jiten [*Dictionary of Buddhism and Indian Thought*] (Shunjūsha, Tokyo, 1987).

Index